FAILING IN THE FIELD

To Jeff & Teri —

Who never would have thought of me and "failure" in the same sentence. Infinite thanks & love —

Jake

FAILING IN THE FIELD

WHAT WE CAN LEARN WHEN FIELD RESEARCH GOES WRONG

**DEAN KARLAN AND
JACOB APPEL**

PRINCETON UNIVERSITY PRESS
Princeton & Oxford

Published by Princeton University Press,
41 William Street, Princeton, New Jersey 08540

In the United Kingdom: Princeton University Press,
6 Oxford Street, Woodstock, Oxfordshire OX20 1TR

press.princeton.edu

ISBN 978-0-691-16189-1

Library of Congress Control Number: 2016944394

British Library Cataloging-in-Publication Data is available

This book has been composed in Adobe Text Pro and Replica Bold

Printed on acid-free paper. ∞

Printed in the United States of America

10 9 8 7 6 5 4 3 2 1

WE DEDICATE THIS BOOK

to our failures and our families, which we are glad to say are mutually exclusive. And also to Dudley.

CONTENTS

FAILING IN THE FIELD

WHY FAILURES?

Thomas Edison tried hundreds of materials before discovering that bamboo fiber could serve as a lightbulb filament. When asked how it felt to fail so much, he reportedly answered, "I have not failed 700 times. I have not failed once. I have succeeded in proving that those 700 ways will not work. When I have eliminated the ways that will not work, I will find the way that will work."

We salute Edison and, in creating this book, we drew inspiration from his attitude. Like the lightbulb, knowledge is a product; research produces it. Just as Edison tinkered with his filaments to see which produced a bright and lasting light, researchers tinker with research designs to see which produce meaningful and reliable knowledge. The more experimenters share their private failures so that others can learn, the more quickly we will find the ways that work. This book is an effort to document some of the many research failures in this space so that others, to paraphrase Edison, do not have to re-prove that all those 700 ways do *not* work.

In collecting and reflecting on failures we have vacillated between two guiding thoughts. The first, like the Edison story, is inspirational:

> *Failure is the key to success; each mistake teaches us something.*
> —MORIHEI UESHIBA

Some clichés actually contain good advice. This one happens to be our core motivation for writing this book.

The second mantra, while less sanguine, is no less true:

> *Failure: When Your Best Just Isn't Good Enough*
> —WWW.DESPAIR.COM/PRODUCTS/FAILURE

Every basic textbook in economics teaches why people should ignore sunk costs when making decisions. Yet reality of course is a tad different: people often let sunk costs sway decisions. We must remember that we will all fail here or there, despite our best efforts. Sometimes we just cannot do better. Rather than double down, we may need to learn and move on.

SUCCESS; OR WHY THE FAILURES ARE WORTH THE HASSLE

Today, conversations about poverty alleviation and development are much more focused on evidence than they were before—a shift due, in large part, to the radical drop in the price of data and the growth of randomized controlled trials (RCTs) in the development sector. Long the dominant methodology for determining medical treatments, RCTs found their way into domestic social policy discussions as early as the 1960s when they were used to evaluate government assistance programs, such as negative income tax rates for the poor. In the 1990s, a new crop of development economists began using RCTs in the field to evaluate aid programs. Their work generated enthusi-

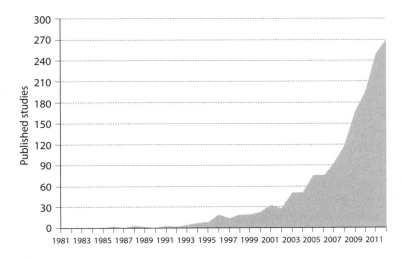

FIGURE 1. Published randomized controlled trials in development, 1981–2013. Drew B. Cameron, Anjini Mishra, and Annette N. Brown, "The Growth of Impact Evaluation for International Development: How Much Have We Learned?" *Journal of Development Effectiveness* 8, no. 1 (2016): 1–21.

asm for the RCT approach and helped spark a pervasive trend, illustrated in figure 1 with data compiled by the International Initiative for Impact Evaluation (3ie), a donor consortium.

PUBLISHED RANDOMIZED CONTROLLED TRIALS IN DEVELOPMENT, 1981—2013

The role of RCTs in development has expanded not just in volume but also in variety. Many early applications were straightforward program evaluations ("What impact did program X have on outcomes Y and Z?"). Now RCTs are commonly used to test specific theories in development, such as whether cognitive attention influences savings and borrowing behavior; whether specific forms of moral hazard are present in credit markets; how social networks influence the adoption of new agricultural technologies among smallholder farmers; whether increasing attention or information can lead to people taking their medication more reliably; and whether a commitment device to invest in fertilizer improves yields for farmers. Finally, RCTs help address operational issues, such as the optimal repayment schedule for a loan, how to price sanitation services, or how to describe cash transfer programs to recipients. Naturally these are not mutually exclusive categories: some RCTs examine the efficacy of a program while successfully testing a theory and answering important operational questions. Such is the aim of many studies, but there is variation in how well a study accomplishes each of the three.

As the number and range of RCTs have grown, so have the quantity and quality of lessons learned. Consequently, policies are changing, too—often slowly and with a lot of pushing, but changing nonetheless. Innovations for Poverty Action (IPA, a nonprofit organization that Dean founded) and MIT's Abdul Latif Jameel Poverty Action Lab (J-PAL) collaborate and keep a tally of such victories from their own collective work, called "scale-ups": cases where social programs were expanded after rigorous evaluation produced strong evidence of effectiveness. The work spans many areas, including education, health, microfinance, income support, and political economy. Here are eight examples:

- Improved targeting and distribution of subsidized rice—65+ million people[1]
- Remedial education with volunteer tutors—47+ million children[2]
- Conditional community block grants—6+ million people[3]
- School-based deworming—95+ million children[4]
- Chlorine dispensers for safe water—7+ million people[5]

- Free distribution of insecticidal bed nets for malaria (*no figure available*)[6]
- Police skills-training to improve investigation quality and victim satisfaction—10 percent of police personnel in Rajasthan, India[7]
- Integrated "Graduation" grants for training, coaching, and financial service programs that aim to increase the income of those in extreme poverty—400,000+ households[8]

The diversity of scale-ups is telling.

On one end of the scale-ups spectrum are tweaks to large, established programs. In these cases, studies found subtle changes to the design or delivery that drastically improved overall program effectiveness. For example, researchers worked with the Indonesian government to add a simple performance incentive to a community block grant program such that communities that achieved better health and education outcomes would receive larger grants for the following year. This drove significant health improvements compared to similar grant amounts given without incentives.[9]

A study of a Colombian government-run conditional monthly cash transfer program found big impacts from *delaying* a portion of the monthly payment until school fees were due the following term. This subtle variation produced the same short-term gains in attendance as did immediate payments but also significantly increased the portion of children who continued on to the next grade. Similarly, delaying payment until high school graduation maintained short-term attendance gains while increasing matriculation in postsecondary education.[10]

Again in Indonesia, another program took on systematic underuse of the government's largest social program, a rice subsidy for its poorest citizens. Only 30 percent of eligible households knew about the program, and among those who did, many were confused about the price and the subsidy amount to which they were entitled. An evaluation tested the impact of two interventions: distributing personal ID cards that included price and quantity information and served to remind people they were eligible for the subsidy; and a community-based awareness campaign. Both proved highly effective in getting eligible people to use the program and in combating overcharging. For an additional cost of about $2.40 per household, they increased the average value of the subsidy by more than $12.[11]

Finally, insecticidal bed nets have long been used to fight malaria, but until recently there was no consensus about pricing. Some felt they should be given away for free—this way nobody would be priced out of protection. Others felt recipients should pay *something*, reasoning that a free handout would more likely be forgotten or neglected than would an intentional investment. Evaluation provided critical guidance: When offered for free in Kenya, bed nets reached far more people and were equally likely to be used properly.[12] Free distribution is now endorsed by the UK's Department for International Development, the UN Millennium Project, and other leading organizations.

On the other end of the scale-ups spectrum are big program evaluations that then lead to entire programs being scaled. Three examples are remedial education with volunteer tutors,[13] chlorine dispensers for safe water,[14] and an integrated multifaceted grant program (often called a "Graduation" program) to increase income for those in extreme poverty.[15] In these cases, the initial evaluations were focused on trying something new or something without solid evidence rather than fine-tuning existing approaches. These programs began as limited-scale pilots and grew as repeated rounds of evaluation confirmed their effectiveness.

Remedial education with tutors began as a 200-school pilot in the Indian state of Gujarat and now reaches nearly 34 million students across the country. Taken together, the scale-ups on IPA and J-PAL's list reach over 200 million people in the developing world.

Chlorine dispensers for safe water address a simple and pervasive problem. Adding a few drops of chlorine is a cheap, effective, and widely available way to sterilize drinking water that might otherwise make people sick; but usage rates are low, even among those who know about chlorine disinfectant, have access, and would benefit from using it. A potential solution sprang from the behavioral insight that people might be more likely to use chlorine if it were available "just-in-time," at the moment when they collected the water. Voilà: Chlorine dispensers were installed next to wells and community water taps. This also lowered cost, as there was only one end-node per village that needed replenishing with chlorine. A series of evaluations confirmed the positive health impact of the dispensers and helped drive scale-up. As of the end of 2015, some 7.6 million individuals in East Africa use clean water thanks to this simple solution.

A more recent example is cash transfer programs that give money directly to the poor to use however they see fit. Initially such programs were met with skepticism. Many wondered whether the poor would use the money wisely. But an RCT of a cash transfer program in Kenya, administered by the nonprofit GiveDirectly, found large impacts on recipients' incomes, assets, food consumption, psychological well-being, and more.[16] Encouraged by the evidence, the philanthropic funding organization Good Ventures gave $25 million to GiveDirectly to expand its programs. Based on these early results, other countries are expanding their own cash transfer programs. Many questions remain about how best to design these programs, but they do provide a useful benchmark for comparison. We might now ask of any poverty alleviation program that requires funding, "Does it do better than just giving that money directly to the poor?"

Cash transfers could be thought of as what-to-do-when-you-do-not-know-what-else-to-do. But they are not a panacea; many problems of poverty are not simply a by-product of having less money. Had this been true, redistributive policies would have solved many problems long ago. There are likely many market failures present: low information for the poor or lack of access to markets, for example. This implies that efforts that tackle market failures, perhaps along with redistribution, may have a multiplicative effect that mere redistribution does not have. In other words, transfer $1 of cash and the recipient gets $1 (actually about $0.95, which is quite good). But maybe there are ways of transferring $1 along with $0.50 of services that then generates $2 for the recipient. That is a bigger bang for your buck (or buck-fifty). To examine that, we turn to the last example, a "Graduation" program designed to help build income for families in extreme poverty.

Researchers from IPA and J-PAL completed a six-country evaluation of a Graduation program that provides families with comprehensive assistance, including a productive asset (e.g., four goats), training to care for the asset, basic nutrition and health care support, access to savings, and life-skills coaching. The theory is that such coordinated, multilayered support helps families graduate to self-sufficiency. The evaluation followed some 21,000 of the world's poorest people, over three years, and found strong positive social returns ranging from 133 to 433 percent. That is, the program generated between $1.33 and $4.33 in increased consumption for the household for each dollar spent.

The Graduation study is a breakthrough in scale and coordination. Following individuals over three years is a challenge in itself. Doing so across six countries (Ethiopia, Ghana, Honduras, India, Pakistan, and Peru); asking comparable questions in six languages; measuring and comparing social and financial outcomes across six economies with regional currencies, prices, and staple goods; and working with six different implementation teams was an even bigger undertaking.

Replications usually happen one by one, if at all. One successful study might generate interest (and funding) for a replication, so it often takes years to build up a body of evidence around a particular program or approach. With the Graduation study researchers have evidence from six settings all at once (and a seventh, from Bangladesh, conducted by separate researchers), enabling them to see differences across contexts. It brings us closer to understanding *how* Graduation programs truly work—and for whom and under what conditions they might work best.

This all makes the Graduation study sound like a blistering success, but there were failures here, too. There were some simple "oops" mistakes: for example, leaving out a module in a survey, and then having no measure of mental health in a round of data. Many outcome measures were, upon reflection, not as comparable across sites as researchers would have liked. Other challenges were inevitable consequences of differences across countries, say, in researchers' abilities to ask detailed questions about the costs of rearing an animal. Finally, each site made huge promises to deliver detailed monitoring data in order to help capture contextual differences between the six settings, but none of these data became available in the end, rendering comparisons across sites more challenging.

Academic journals and media reports are now full of success stories of rigorous evidence being brought to the fight against poverty. IPA and J-PAL have been featured in major news outlets of all stripes, from *Time*, TED, and the *New Yorker* to the *Economist* and the *Wall Street Journal*. Despite all the good press, not everything is rosy. We believe sharing the studies that are not fit for the *New York Times*—the ones that will otherwise just die, undocumented, in the memory of the researchers—can yield valuable lessons.

We also had a deeper motivation in writing this book: Researchers must begin talking about failures to ensure evidence plays an *appropriate* role in policy. The language of RCTs as the "gold standard" for evidence has no doubt helped fuel their rise. But it is telling that one rarely hears RCT researchers make such claims; there is a risk of overreaching. The fact is, where it is appropriate to use, a well-executed RCT will provide the strongest evidence of causality. It will say, more decisively and precisely than other methods, whether program X caused outcome Y for the population being studied. Much of this nuance gets lost in public discussion. All too often, what comes through is just that RCT equals gold standard. But the "where it is appropriate" and "well-executed" parts are equally important! Not every program or theory is amenable to study by an RCT; even when one is, the RCT can be poorly executed, producing no valuable knowledge. (Read on for many such examples.)

In fact, there is meta-evidence that employing poor methods is correlated with biased results. In an analysis of medical RCTs, researchers found that studies with either inadequate or unclear concealment of assignment to treatment and control had larger treatment effects. This is a striking result that has one obvious and one less-than-obvious interpretation. The obvious: poor methods lead to higher variance in outcomes or, worse, suggest possible manipulation. Thus they generate a higher proportion with statistically significant treatment effects, and in general larger treatment effects get published. The less-than-obvious: perhaps journal editors and referees are more likely to overlook sloppy methods when the treatment effects are large.

They are inclined to be fastidious about borderline results but do not want nitpicky details to get in the way of reporting "big" results. Alas, to test between these two explanations one ideally would randomly assign the use of sloppy methods to journal submissions to see whether the sloppy methods affected acceptance rates differentially for high and low treatment effect papers—hardly a feasible study.

Bottom line, a bad RCT can be worse than doing no study at all: it teaches us little, uses up resources that could be spent on providing more services (even if of uncertain value), likely sours people on the notion of RCTs and research in general, and if believed may even steer us in the wrong direction. Naturally the same can be said about any poorly designed or poorly executed research study.

OUR FOCUS IN THIS BOOK

Even in the relatively confined space of international development research, there are many different kinds of failures. We will not attempt to address, or even describe, them all. Let us say more about what we will and will not discuss.

What we do focus on in this book are *research failures*, cases where a study is conceived with a particular question in mind (e.g., "Does financial literacy training help borrowers repay their microloans?") but does not manage to answer it. Why might this happen? Such cases fall into two categories. Either researchers started out with a faulty plan, or they had a good plan but were derailed by events that took place once the study was underway. The kinds of failures we discuss in chapters 1 and 2, research setting and technical design, fall into the first category. The second category includes partner organization challenges, survey and measurement execution problems, and low participation rates, which we discuss in chapters 3, 4, and 5.

In contrast, sometimes a product or service (e.g., micro-loans, scholarships, vaccinations) is delivered as planned, and then a well-executed evaluation returns a precise null result—statistical confirmation that the intervention did not causally influence target outcomes. Simply put, the program did not work. We call such cases *idea failures*. These are important lessons to learn and to share. But they are not our subject here.

Many idea failures are actually research successes. With a precisely estimated result of "no impact" in hand, one can confidently move on and try other approaches. The only real failure we see in these scenarios is with the academic publishing system: precise "no impact" results are often rejected by scholarly journals, an embarrassing and pernicious reality. Many are trying to address this, but, to mix bad metaphors, it is a bit like trying to herd cats in an effort to move Sisyphus's rock. A good aspiration for an evaluation is to shed light on *why* something works, not merely whether it works. Idea failures can be just as revealing as successes: if the approach seemed sensible, why did it not work? "No impact" results notwithstanding, if a study can explain that, then the publishing system should reward it just as it rewards research documenting ideas that work.

WHAT IS IN THE REST OF THE BOOK

In part 1 (chapters 1–5) we sort research failures into five broad categories, describing how and why they might arise and highlighting common instances or subtypes of each. The categories are as follows: inappropriate research setting, technical design flaws, partner organization challenges, survey and measurement execution problems, and low participation rates. Occasionally we illustrate these with hypotheticals (e.g., "Imagine you are evaluating a school feeding program in 200 schools . . ."), but where possible we include actual examples from the field.

In part 2 (chapters 6–11) we present case studies of six failed projects in more detail, including background and motivation, study design and implementation plan, what exactly went wrong, and lessons learned. These are forensic-style reports on projects that genuinely flopped. Like most instances that call for forensics, the cases they describe are messy and multifaceted, with each touching on multiple failure types. Indeed, one lesson that emerged as we wrote and compiled these cases is that individual failures tend to snowball quickly, especially if they are not caught and addressed immediately. It is worth mentioning that many of the cases in part 2 deal with "microcredit plus" programs—that is, programs that seek to bundle some additional services along with microloans. This similarity across cases is partly a consequence of the simple fact that we (particularly Dean) have done a lot of research on microfinance. But while these cases are programmatically similar, each one failed in its own special way and for its own special reasons. This is, in itself, an interesting finding: the potential pitfalls of research depend not just on the program being studied but on many other factors, too. Conversely, studies of vastly different kinds of programs can fail in similar ways and for similar reasons.

Finally, the conclusion and appendix distill key lessons and themes from across the cases discussed in parts 1 and 2 and offer some guidance for those about to embark on their own field studies. By this point, you will have read a fair bit about what not to do. But what *do* you do? The advice there hardly amounts to a comprehensive guide, but it is a start. In addition to providing positive takeaways from cases in this book, we also point to external resources that provide concrete guidelines, procedures, and strategies to help researchers design and run successful field studies.

WHAT IS BEYOND THIS BOOK

We are glad and grateful that dozens of colleagues, from first-time research assistants to tenured professors, have joined in this effort, publicly sharing their own difficult experiences so that others can benefit. But alas, the field of international development research lacks a tradition of talking openly about failures. Finding willing contributors was difficult—which is one reason why many of the examples we discuss here are our own.

In writing this book, we reached out to more researchers than are featured in these pages. Many admired the venture but had no story they were willing to share publicly. Some had concerns about the sensitivities of funders or partner organizations that had been involved in failed research efforts (especially if they hoped to work with those funders or partners again in the future); others were reluctant to cast as "failures" studies that had significant hiccups but still produced some publishable results. Perhaps some simply did not want their name on a list of researchers who made mistakes.

Given the realities of funding, publication, and career advancement these researchers face, their reasons are understandable. It is the expectations placed on them that are unrealistic. Anyone who tries enough times will fail occasionally; why pretend otherwise? The subject need not be taboo. If more researchers make a habit of sharing their failures, the quality of research can improve overall.

This book represents a first step down that path. Beyond the examples in these pages, we are launching, with David McKenzie and Berk Özler of the World Bank, an online companion—an effort to aggregate and categorize failure stories on their moderated blog. Ideally it will become common practice among researchers, when studies go bad, to briefly capture what went wrong and share it with the community. If this takes off, we will then work with them to launch the failure repository as a stand-alone site. Equally important, we hope researchers embarking on new studies genuinely use the resource to look at past failures, incorporate relevant lessons, and avoid learning the hard way themselves.

PART I

LEADING CAUSES OF RESEARCH FAILURES

CHAPTER 1

INAPPROPRIATE RESEARCH SETTING

MANTRA: *Thou shalt have a well-understood context and an intervention that maps sensibly to a plausible theory of change.*

How is a research study and evaluation born? One policy-driven story proceeds as follows: Begin with observation of a problem or challenge; collaborate with informed constituents who have local knowledge; form theories and hypotheses about the cause of the problem; collect diagnostic information; conceive an intervention that may correct the problem; test it; lastly, iterate, tinker, continue testing, all with an eye to learning how to scale. In cases like these, appropriateness of setting is not a question. The entire research process arises from, and is crafted around, the particular context where the problem exists.

This is a nice plan, but not all research follows it. Hypotheses and intervention ideas often originate elsewhere—perhaps they are extensions or consequences of an existing theory, or inspired by results from other research or from experiences in neighboring countries or countries far away. In such cases, researchers with theories or hypotheses already in hand set out to search for appropriate sites to run experiments. As they consider alternatives, they often look for goodness-of-fit on a variety of key characteristics.

First, researchers must verify that the people in the proposed sample frame are actually facing the problem or challenge to which the intervention is a possible answer. This may seem obvious, but in practice it is not always evident. Imagine an informational public health campaign that told people about the importance of sleeping under bed nets. Ideally, you would try to test such a campaign where the information about bed nets is genuinely *new*. But without a costly pre-survey, how could you tell whether people already know about them?

Second, researchers often seek out partner organizations that can help develop or deliver interventions. Such partners must be both willing and able to participate. In the chapter on partner organization challenges, we will say more about what constitutes "willing and able." In terms of a research setting, the key consideration is that all interventions under study are sufficiently developed and standardized to permit a fair and consistent test. Embarking on a rigorous impact evaluation with a partner that is still tinkering with its product or process can be disastrous. (Side note to avoid confusion: a common misunderstanding is that in order to do an RCT one must make sure that the actual delivery of a service is homogeneous across all treatment recipients. This is not the case. Take, for example, community-driven development programs. In such programs the *process* is static, but what happens in each village is not— and that is fine. One can evaluate whether that process works to generate higher community cohesion, better provision of public goods, etc. It is important to remember that one is then not testing the impact of building health clinics, if that happens to be a public good some communities choose to build; rather one is testing the impact of the *process* of community-driven development.)

Where to draw the line between the tinkering stage and firmly established is not so well-defined. Implementers always face a natural learning curve, commit forgivable beginner's mistakes, and need to make adjustments on the fly—all of which can wreak havoc when research requires steadfast adherence to experimental protocols. A guiding principle: the intervention should be well-enough defined such that if it works, it is clear what "it" is that could then be replicated or scaled.

Finally, researchers must look at physical, social, and political features of the setting. First, these should fit the intervention and the theory that underlies it. Here is an obvious one: tests of malaria prevention programs should only be undertaken in areas where malaria is prevalent. A less obvious one: suppose we want to test the impact of timely market price information on farmers' decisions about where to sell their produce. Such a study should be conducted only where farmers genuinely have choices—where there are multiple markets within reasonable travel distance, and those markets allow new entrants, and so forth. Even if we do not see farmers switching markets beforehand, that does not imply they are unable to do so; indeed, their mobility may be revealed by doing the study. Second, context must permit delivery of the intervention. Studying the impact of an in-school reproductive health class likely will not work if talking about sex is taboo. Finally, data collection needs to be possible, whether through survey (Are people willing to talk honestly?) or administrative data (Are institutions willing to share proprietary information?).

In practice, choosing a setting is often a complex process. It takes time and effort, judgment, and a theory that describes *how* the underlying context will interact with the treatment to be tested.

Problems often arise when researchers try to shoehorn a fit. It is natural, when almost all criteria are met, to convince oneself that "we are close enough"—and especially tempting to do so if considerable resources have already been sunk into the work. In such cases it is easy to become fixated on "getting it done" or credulous that potential obstacles will work themselves out. Beware.

Ultimately this is about risk management. These are not binary and certain conditions in the world. Rather, much of the process relies on trust and judgment. There are a few common pitfalls worth mentioning.

POORLY TIMED STUDIES

Concurrent events, though unrelated to the study, sometimes alter the environment in ways that can compromise research. It could be a change in anything—politics, technology, weather, policy. Such a change arrives as a potential wrinkle in an otherwise well-considered plan. With staff committed, partners on board, and funding lined up, researchers rarely feel they have the luxury to wait and see what happens.

In a study we will see in chapter 9, researchers studied a microcredit product in India that involved borrowers buying chicks from a supplier, raising them, and selling the grown chickens to a distributor. A tight schedule had been created for the supplier and distributor to visit borrowers' villages on pre-specified dates, making drop-offs and pickups in a flatbed truck. But a software upgrade for the microlender, unrelated to the research, took far longer than expected and delayed the launch of the study until the beginning of the Indian monsoon season. Daily rains would make some roads impassable, throwing a wrench in the distribution schedule, and would also make it more difficult for clients to raise chickens in the first place.

At this point, the study had already been considerably delayed but researchers decided to press on—a mistake in hindsight.

Similarly, in chapter 10 we discuss a study with a microlender in which loan officers were tasked with delivering health and business training to clients as they repaid their loans. Shortly before the study began, and again unrelated to the research, the lender changed a policy for first-time borrowers. Instead of receiving twenty-four hours of new client orientation (much of which was spent driving home the importance of making payments on time), they shortened the program to eight hours. Though the nuts and bolts of the loan product remained the same, repayment rates for new clients fell immediately following the change. Loan officers found themselves forced to split their limited time between chasing down payments from delinquent clients and delivering health and business training modules, a tension that (along with other issues) ultimately doomed the study.

TECHNICALLY INFEASIBLE INTERVENTIONS

Many studies rely on infrastructure—roads, power grids, cold chains for medicine—simply to deliver treatment. Researchers can verify directly whether these things exist and how reliable they are, but doing so takes time and resources. Such investigation may seem unnecessary, especially when local forecasts are optimistic. The power is always supposed to come back on— next week. Partner staff will say with certainty, "Everyone here has a phone." If the study depends on it, do not take anybody's word for it. Get the data, either from a reliable third party or, better yet, by surveying directly.

Alternatively, learn the hard way. In a study we discuss in chapter 6, Peruvian microfinance bank Arariwa took clients through a multimedia financial literacy training program that included short DVD-based segments. Hoping to avoid the expense of buying all new equipment, the researchers had asked the loan officers who would do the training (and who had been working with these clients for years) whether they would be able to borrow TVs and DVD players from friends, family, or clients. The loan officers were confident they could, so the project went ahead without new equipment. Turns out audio/video setups are harder to come by in rural Peru than the loan officers had suspected; an audit midway through the project revealed that almost none of the loan officers had succeeded in showing clients the DVD segments.

IMMATURE PRODUCTS

Interventions tested with RCTs often have some novel features: they are additions or tweaks to existing programs or products, expansions to new sites, or new approaches altogether. Such novelty might be precisely what makes for an interesting study. But it also makes it hard to predict what will happen when the intervention lands in the field.

Starting an evaluation too soon—that is, launching before the team has thoroughly kicked the tires on the product or program under study—can be a mistake. On this front, both researchers and partner organizations often fall prey to overconfidence or to false optimism. Most of the details are settled and the outstanding questions that remain may not seem major at the time. The implementers may bring a wealth of relevant experience to the table and may also be able to draw on lessons from similar programs run in similar settings. But experience suggests that each new implementation brings its own unique, and potentially disruptive, wrinkles.

In a case we will see in chapter 7, a microlender in Ghana partnered with researchers to study the relationship between interest rates and client demand for microloans. (As a side note, this project is actually how the coauthors of this book met. Jacob was the research assistant for Dean and others back in 2006, helping to launch this study—a tad earlier than we should have.) The lender, which had previously made only traditional group-based loans, created its first individual-based micro-loan product for the study and conceived a direct marketing campaign to invite prospective clients to apply. Door-to-door marketing was a new tactic for the lender, and they wisely ran a pre-pilot to test it before launch. Because the new product was similar in many ways to its predecessors, and because experienced staff would be handling it, the research team deemed it unnecessary to extend the pre-pilot to include loan application and administration. But this proved to be a mistake, as seemingly minor changes in the application process created major operational delays.

In another case, discussed in chapter 11, two established Indian firms, a microlender and an insurer, teamed up to bundle a rudimentary insurance policy with the lender's microloans. All parties suspected that fairly priced insurance would be an appealing perk and make for a more desirable product, so they launched it sight unseen. It turned out clients saw it as a burden—an unexpected reaction that completely undermined the study.

RESEARCHERS NOT KNOWING WHEN TO WALK AWAY

Researchers are like hopeful hikers in a mountain cabin. The idea—the peak—is there, beckoning through the window. In the previous examples, they are impetuous, setting off with imperfect knowledge of the terrain and weather forecast, in spite of (or ignorant of) the hazards that might await them. Once on the trail, they find an environment more hostile than they expected. In the cases presented in part 2, we will detail their encounters with rain and sleet, rockslides, impassable crevasses, and the like.

What if the weather is so bad they cannot even open the cabin door? As in the other examples, the hikers are committed and eager, and loathe to give up: they have already obtained their permits, invested in gear, and come a long way to the park. Rather than a fight against the elements, though, they find themselves in a war of attrition. How long will they hold out for a chance at the summit? When is the right time to cut their losses, pack up the car, and head back down the mountain?

Researchers Billy Jack of Georgetown University, Tavneet Suri of MIT, and Chris Woodruff of the University of Warwick lived this dilemma through a study about supply-chain credit. They had partnered with a local bank and a consumer product distributor to create a loan product that allowed retailers to purchase additional inventory from the distributor on credit, all using mobile phones. Having the partners on board was an achievement in itself: both were established, experienced firms with the capacity to deliver such a product and with footprints large enough to support a robust test of it. With an implementation plan in place, research staff on the ground, and agreements signed by all parties, it appeared everyone was ready to set out for the summit.

But every time they circled up for a final gear check, they found something was out of place. First, the bank discovered its back-end system could not accommodate the structure of the product to which everyone had initially agreed. This realization prompted a second round of discussions, after which the research team submitted a new product proposal that remained true to the initial terms and fit the bank's back end. The bank considered this for a few months and finally wrote back with changes that differed from both the initial agreement and the second discussions. A third set of meetings reconciled these differences and set in place a revised implementation plan. As the launch date neared, the research team requested screenshots of the bank's back-end software to verify the product terms had been set as agreed and discovered that the bank had raised the interest rate of the loan significantly. (The minutes the bank had recorded from the previous meeting, including an agreement on an interest rate, differed from what had actually been discussed.) This prompted a fourth meeting, which produced another revised plan, including a limited pilot to start immediately. The pilot quickly ran into technical issues with the software that supported mobile phone integration, rendering the product unviable and forcing them to pause the project again.

Amid all the false starts, the research team had recruited participants and run three separate baseline surveys, all of which had to be scrapped when launch was delayed once more. Getting the picture? The whole saga took nearly three years to unfold; cost countless hours of planning, re-planning, and negotiation from researchers and partners alike; and produced nothing but frustration. Along the way, the researchers could see their chances were narrowing. More than once they considered shutting down the project, but there always seemed to be a glimmer of hope that encouraged them to try again or hold another meeting with the partner. The longer they stayed, the more invested they became, and the more painful (and wasteful) an exit appeared.

At some level this is a straightforward story of failing to acknowledge sunk cost—doubling down in an effort to capitalize on expenditures of time and resources that cannot be recovered. Though we may understand intellectually that continuing is futile, the inclination to do so still persists. We do not want our work to go to waste. Paradoxically, of all the intellectual challenges that arise in the course of designing and implementing a rigorous research study, the greatest may be deciding when to pull the plug.

CHAPTER 2

TECHNICAL DESIGN FLAWS

MANTRA: *Thou shalt attend to technical but important details like survey design, timing, sample size requirements, and randomization protocols.*

Researchers design RCTs to test specific theories, often by examining the impacts of specific interventions. The guts of experimental design—the mechanics of randomization, statistical power and necessary sample size calculations, construction of surveys and other data collection tools—are mainly steps along the way. If they are carried out properly and do not present any unexpected problems, they are usually omitted from the academic papers that arise from such studies. This is partly because the details are too numerous to include every one and partly because researchers are directed by reviewers to remove them or shift them to online appendices to keep articles from getting too long. The theoretical and policy-relevant results take center stage, and the rest fades into the background.

Although they are relatively unsung, these details matter. A lot.

SURVEY DESIGN ERRORS

What researchers want to know often seems so straightforward: What was the revenue of this business last week? How
many people live in your household? These feel like factual
questions with well-defined terms and discrete, knowable answers. But then one starts asking these questions of real people,
and all sorts of unexpected complexities arise. Last week's business revenue? "That depends if we should include purchases
made on credit and in-kind trades. How do we value in-kind
trades, anyway?" Head count for a household? "Well, there are
five in the main house, and my son stays here sometimes but
goes to the city to work during the winter. Does he count? Also,
my sister and her husband and child have been staying in the
back house for the past eight months rent free. But sometimes
they pitch in for food. Do they count?"

Even the simplest questions are often fraught. It is not just
what is asked but how it is asked that matters. The wording
of the questions; who does the asking, and to whom; the response scale provided; the order in which response options
appear; the placement of questions in a module and modules
in a survey—all these have the potential to push responses one
way or another. One is reminded of the admonition for policy
design from Richard Thaler and Cass Sunstein's *Nudge* (2009)
that there is no "neutral" option in setting up a policy (or, in this
case, a survey); every alternative has consequences. The full set
of considerations is too long to list here, and in any event this
book is not meant to be a holistic guide to survey design. We
will mention just two common issues to avoid.

The first is bloated surveys, particularly without a clear analysis plan for all questions. When researchers have doubts about
a question—Does this really get at the desired piece of data?
Is it too noisy a measure?—it is often tempting to add another

question that is similar (but not totally redundant) as a kind of double check. After all, a team will already be in the field and conducting surveys; what are a few more questions? The same reasoning applies to items not immediately relevant to key outcomes of interest in the study. Including one more question always seems like cheap insurance. It is easy to imagine the unhappy alternative: What if omitting the question means missing out on an important piece of data? There is unlikely to be an easy second chance to get it.

One cost of additional questions, often hard to observe, is survey fatigue. Respondents get tired, decline to answer questions, and give inconsistent responses. (The quality of surveyors' work often suffers, too.) A second cost comes later: What exactly is the analysis plan? How will one decide which question is better? Or is the plan merely to average the two, arbitrarily?

The second issue is poorly designed survey items. Common culprits include poorly defined terms and vague or ambiguous questions, open to multiple interpretations. Translating surveys by non-native speakers into local languages or dialects often further complicates matters. Especially if combined with imperfect surveyor training, these can create high variation in responses across surveyors. Inadequate response scales are another common misstep. Each question must be able to accommodate the full range of answers surveyors will receive in the field. This is not generally an issue for free-response questions, where any answer can be entered as text (or numbers), but it can be a problem for multiple-choice questions where the survey designer must anticipate and list out all plausible answers.

Take the following example, from a 2012 project in Ghana. Researchers Günther Fink of Harvard University and Dean Karlan and Chris Udry of Yale University wanted to find out whether respondents were sleeping under insecticide-treated bed nets, a key preventative measure against malaria. Their survey asked:

Q1) Do you own an insecticide-treated bed net?
    a. Yes
    b. No [if No, skip Q2]

Q2) "Can you show me your bed net?" [surveyor to directly observe respondent's sleeping area and record the appropriate response below]
    a. Does not actually own a bed net
    b. Has a bed net but it is not hung
    c. Has a bed net that is hung

The options seemed straightforward—until surveyors in the field encountered a scenario that did not fit. Quite a few respondents, it turned out, did own bed nets and had hung them in their bedrooms, but over the doorway instead of over the bed. Surveyors were not sure whether to record such cases as (b) or (c). Fortunately the problem was caught during the first two days of surveying by a research assistant auditing surveys in the field, and the research team quickly added a fourth response option to Q2. (This underscores one of the key themes of this book: the importance of well-trained and careful staff to help manage the intricacies of fieldwork.)

The lesson: field test survey questions before launch. Also, debrief regularly with field survey teams to find out which questions respondents are struggling with, which parts of the survey are hardest to administer, and the like. Watch for questions coming back with high rates of "other" or "N/A" responses checked. Changing the survey midstream is not ideal, but it may be necessary if respondents or surveyors are consistently having difficulty with some parts.

INADEQUATE MEASUREMENT PROTOCOL

No less important than the survey and other data collection tools is the plan to deploy them. Again, unexpected complications emerge from seemingly straightforward tasks as they are repeated hundreds or thousands of times in challenging field environments.

Researchers' first order of business is ensuring that they truly understand and follow their chosen process for inclusion so they can be confident they are collecting data from the right people. Typically this means either confirming that potential respondents meet some specific criteria (e.g., they are full-time produce sellers in a specific market area, or taxi drivers who work nights) or matching names on a roster (e.g., when a microlender provides a list of its clients). If it is the former, surveyors find themselves in the role of census workers, trying to suss out the details of a person's life and making judgments on the fly. (Suppose a woman sells vegetables in this market eight months per year, sells cloth from the same market stall two months a year, and returns to her village two months a year, leaving her daughter to mind the stall. Is she a full-time produce seller?) If it is the latter, surveyors must confirm respondents' identities. Sometimes this is as simple as asking a name directly or checking an ID; other times it is more complex. In some cases researchers can use security questions for verification— for instance, asking for respondents' birthdates or home-towns—if respondents have provided that information earlier during a baseline or intake survey.

Robust identity verification is especially important when there is a compelling reason to participate in a survey, for example, if the study itself is perceived as valuable or prestigious or if respondents are being compensated. In chapter 8 we will discuss a study in Uganda where the survey included a game played with real money, through which participants could earn up to a couple of dollars. Small as it was, that amount proved sufficiently enticing that people began posing as the rightful subjects to get a piece of the action.

Indeed, the question of whether, how, and how much to compensate respondents is complicated. For example, there is an ethical consideration: if people (especially needy people) are taking time away from productive activities to participate in research, some argue they should be made whole. But there is a strategic dimension, too, with implications for data quality. If the hassle of participating far outweighs the benefits, nobody will opt in; if the benefits far outweigh the hassle, people might opt in for the wrong reasons and try to stay in the surveyor's good graces, often by saying whatever they think the researchers want to hear.

Another question is when and where to carry out the survey. Will respondents be interviewed at home, at work, or in a neutral location? Can a spouse, child, or friend listen in, or will the survey be completely private? Setting can affect responses. If surveyors shadow respondents during the workday to minimize inconvenience, they often face divided attention; alternatively, if respondents have to miss work for a survey they are often in a hurry to finish. For some kinds of questions, asking in public dissuades a respondent from lying, lest his neighbor overhear and call his bluff; for other questions the effect is exactly the opposite.

The situation is not hopeless. The choices researchers make—what they ask, how they ask it, who does the asking, when and where—have myriad and subtle consequences; but one can make better (or worse) choices. The best advice is to try to understand those consequences by field testing or piloting surveys and protocols if possible and to consider them when deciding how to proceed.

MISTAKES IN RANDOMIZATION, POWER, AND NECESSARY SAMPLE SIZE CALCULATIONS

These bedrock components of RCT design are unique neither to field research nor to international development. In lab settings, they are almost always managed directly by researchers. But when, in the course of field research, partners are engaged in marketing, delivery of products and services, and data collection, they sometimes fall out of researchers' control, as the following example illustrates.

Dean Karlan and Daniel Wood of Clemson University were working with the nonprofit Freedom From Hunger on a fundraising study that tested the efficacy of two different kinds of direct mail solicitations.[1] They planned a simple horse race: randomly assign potential donors to receive one of the two solicitations and see which generated more giving. Freedom From Hunger engaged a marketing firm to manage the direct mail campaign, gave them a list of past donors' addresses, and instructed them to randomly assign each name to one of the two solicitations. The envelopes went out on schedule. Unbeknownst to the researchers, they were not truly randomized. With almost perfect consistency, more recent donors had received one kind of solicitation, less recent ones the other. Apparently the marketing firm had (roughly) sorted the list by date of last donation and split it in half. The top half got one kind of flyer, and the bottom half got the other.

This ruined the test. The first sign that something was amiss was the incredibly big treatment effect: it was twenty times the level that had been seen in an earlier round of the study. This told the researchers something was likely wrong, which prompted them to go back to the donor list and discover what had happened. In the end, it was clear that the timing of the last gift was a huge driver of the timing of the next, and the so-called

randomization was worthless (it was far from random!). There
was nothing to do except throw away the data and add a footnote to the paper. (Applied econometricians may be wondering
whether the researchers could have used a regression discon-
tinuity approach. The answer is that there were not enough
data at the threshold to do so. It also felt deeply odd to write
a paper that used a non-randomized approach to study the
impact on donations of including results from a randomized
trial in fund-raising materials. It did make for a funny footnote,
however.)

The lesson here is simple: watch these steps closely, especially if they are being executed by partners unfamiliar with
randomization.

* * *

Even when researchers do manage these steps directly, there
are some common pitfalls to avoid. Power and necessary sample size calculations rely on parameters that are hard to observe
or guess. As we will see in the chapter on low participation
rates, partners and researchers routinely overestimate take-up
rates (and, consequently, power). Another important param-
eter in many field RCTs is intracluster correlation: the degree
to which individuals within a "cluster" (often a village within
a region or a classroom within a school) behave alike. This is
almost impossible to observe directly, yet researchers must
make some guess—or guesses. The best advice is to run these
calculations multiple times, imagining a range of scenarios in
the field and using a corresponding range of values for key parameters. Rather than offering a single answer—which is likely
to be wrong in any event—this approach will provide some
intuition about the sensitivity of power to changes in levels of
take-up, intracluster correlation, and the like.

One special case worth mentioning is that of heterogeneous treatment effects, when the impact of an intervention on recipients differs according to another variable—for example, when a treatment affects women differently than men. Although heterogeneous treatment effects are often interesting from a theory or policy perspective, they are rarely the focus in experimental design. Instead, researchers usually power their experiments to detect "main effects," a measurement that simply compares the whole treatment group with the whole control group, pooling across all other variables. Powering for heterogeneous treatment effects usually requires a larger study: because the expected difference in impacts of treatment across groups is typically smaller than the expected difference between treatment and control, the necessary sample size is bigger.

Most studies are *not* designed around heterogeneity, yet people often want to understand how well interventions work for different types of participants. Microcredit is a perfect example of this. Although the general question "What is the impact on average for recipients of microcredit?" is important, very little existing research has asked, with precision, "What is the difference between the impact on men and the impact on women?" Two studies by Dean Karlan and Jonathan Zinman in South Africa make this point saliently, one in South Africa (2010) and one in the Philippines (2011). While both studies found various impacts from microcredit on average, many policy conversations immediately zoomed in to focus on differential treatment effects for men and women—about which the studies had little to say. This is not a failure per se in that the general question was the target of the research. The mistake that often happens here is in the interpretation: in testing for heterogeneity, not finding statistically significant differences between groups, and then erroneously concluding "no heterogeneity," when in fact the confidence intervals are quite big and the right answer is closer to "we cannot say anything at all about heterogeneity."

* * *

A notable exception to the general rule of heterogeneity requiring larger samples is the case when an intervention has opposite impacts on different people. For the sake of illustration, suppose we have a (simplistic) theory that says women use money for things that benefit their families like food and medicine, while men are louts who spend every spare cent on alcohol and gambling. Now imagine a program that simply offers cash stipends to supplement income: if given to women, we would expect to see household outcomes improve as families eat well and stay healthy; if given to men, the opposite might happen as husbands fall into debt and addiction. If we then offered such a program to a mix of men and women and ran an RCT, we would have relatively low power for pooled analysis: changes for the better and for the worse would counterbalance and would be on average negative, zero, or positive, all depending simply on the proportion of men and women in the study. In this case a test for heterogeneous effects by gender could have higher power for a given sample size. (Fortunately this is merely a hypothetical example. The evidence on this particular thought exercise is actually more rosy: an RCT conducted with GiveDirectly and IPA in Kenya found no increase in expenditures on alcohol or tobacco for either gender and indeed similar treatment effects regardless of whether money was transferred to the woman or the man in the household [Haushofer and Shapiro 2013].)

On the technical aspects of power and sample size calculations, we refer readers to Rachel Glennerster and Kudzai Takavarasha's book *Running Randomized Evaluations: A Practical Guide*. When considering how to execute a successful experiment, we recall the sage advice given to tailors and carpenters: measure twice, cut once. Check to ensure these steps are done right before proceeding or risk learning the hard way.

CHAPTER 3

PARTNER ORGANIZATION CHALLENGES

MANTRA: *Thou shalt have a willing and able implementing partner.*

Researchers often strive to do studies whose results can directly help policymakers, governments, and organizations decide how to design programs and allocate resources. Occasionally that entails testing ideas or theories in the abstract—with laboratory experiments, for instance—but the laboratory only goes so far when studying human behavior and when trying to inform public policies. Most of the research in this space considers development programs in situ, as they are delivered to real beneficiaries in the field. That usually means working with partner organizations—the nonprofits, civil sector organizations, and government agencies that develop and run those programs.

Why are such organizations willing to join forces with academics, often adding to their responsibilities and offering up their staff and resources in the process? For one, they stand to benefit from what is learned. Done well, evaluations provide evidence about effectiveness and impact, which can be used to stretch scarce resources further to help more people and can also attract additional funding to then help even more people. They also offer operational insights that can spur improvements to products and processes. From a researcher's perspective, partnerships with practitioners offer access to the front lines—to the people who live and breathe the issues in question. This is critical for learning what questions are most relevant and appropriate to ask in the first place and for understanding subtle features of local context that would elude even the most thoughtful researchers. They may be able to offer guidance on where, when, and whom to study; how best to approach surveying given language and cultural conventions; and more.

LIMITED FLEXIBILITY AND BANDWIDTH

Along with the mutual benefits of partnerships come unique challenges. Partner organization staff typically have tremendous expertise, but often experimental protocols require making changes to familiar tasks—for example, altering the criteria by which a loan application is assessed or collecting a few pieces of additional data from customers. Seemingly straightforward tweaks to normal procedures often prove difficult to implement. Sometimes these tweaks are actually good for operations, not just research. But behaviors are still hard to change. Old habits die hard.

* * *

The limits of staff flexibility and bandwidth came to life in a 2007 study, when researchers Dean Karlan and Sendhil Mullainathan partnered with Caja Nacional del Sureste (CNS), a cooperative financial institution in southeast Mexico, on a new savings account that encouraged remittance recipients to save more of their incoming transfers. The account, called Tu Futuro Seguro (TFS; "Your Secure Future" in English), had features designed to address some key obstacles to saving:

- *Free and easy sign-up*—the normal $5 opening fee was waived, and clients needed only a Federal Electoral Card (which was required to receive remittances anyway) to enroll;
- *TFS savings promise*—a nonbinding agreement by which clients chose a default amount to save from each remittance they received;
- *TFS savings booklet*—a dedicated paper booklet to track all account transactions separately; and a
- *Promotional magnet*—a refrigerator magnet, with a spot to stick a photo of a family member, given to all clients (whether they opened the special account or not), with the intention of reminding them about the account.

They designed an RCT to test TFS in four branches before scaling it nationwide. Whenever someone came to one of those branches to receive remittances, special software running on the teller's computer randomly assigned the client on the spot to treatment or control. For clients assigned to treatment, the teller explained TFS and invited them to open a TFS account. Those assigned to control were neither told about TFS nor invited to enroll.

For those who went ahead and opened a TFS account, any future remittance receipt would be accompanied by a scripted verbal reminder from the teller: "In accordance with your Tu Futuro Seguro savings promise, $X of this remittance will be transferred into savings. Would you like to increase your savings promise?" Ultimately it was the client's decision. The savings promise was nonbinding, so the client could choose to divert any portion of the remittance to savings—all, nothing, or any amount in between. The critical point is that it was a *default-in* policy: unless the client explicitly chose otherwise, the amount saved would be the same amount specified in the TFS savings promise at account opening.

To familiarize bank staff with all the new procedures—from randomization software to describing, opening, and operating TFS accounts—the research team held at least two training sessions in each of the four branches before implementation began. They also staggered branches' start dates so that a research assistant could monitor in person for the first week at each branch. With everything in place, they began the study.

Despite training and monitoring, problems arose. Some tellers altered the prescribed script or ignored it altogether. Instead of prompting TFS clients "In accordance with your savings promise, $X of this remittance will be transferred to your TFS account," they might say, "Would you like to transfer any of this remittance to your TFS account?" Though the shift was subtle, it left clients in a *default-out* position—that is, diverting none of their remittances unless they spoke up—and might have significantly impacted their choices about saving. Even worse, if tellers were busy, many did not ask at all whether the client wanted to transfer funds to savings.

Why did tellers do this? Some may not have realized how important it was to maintain the *default-in* policy by reading the savings script verbatim. Although the training sessions had covered that point, and even included mock client interactions for tellers to practice, there was a lot of new information to absorb. But in interviews after the fact, some tellers acknowledged they had deviated from the script because it came into conflict with their primary mandate: to serve clients as quickly and efficiently as possible. Easing long lines or handling testy customers sometimes proved more important than following experimental protocol to the letter. The research assistant recalled pulling a teller aside after finding she had skipped over some survey questions with a client. The teller explained: "Here's an indigenous woman who doesn't speak Spanish very well, and she comes in here literally nursing her baby. She's in a hurry. Really. I'm not going to delay her any longer than I need to finish the savings script." Who can blame her? There are ways to make things "default-in" rather than "default-out," but clearly this was not a good approach.

* * *

Whether the intervention being tested is brand-new or a variation on an existing program, research almost always means extra work for partners. In addition to delivering the intervention itself, subjects must be tracked, data audited and entered, and front-line staff managed. Does the partner have people on the payroll working below capacity who could take this on? If not, are they prepared to accommodate the study by reducing or redistributing other responsibilities for staff members involved?

We will see a case in chapter 7 where researchers partnered with a Ghanaian microfinance bank to test client responses to a range of interest rates. The study used a new loan product for individuals, which had a more intensive application process than the group loans that made up the bulk of the bank's portfolio. The loan officers tapped to work on the study were experienced application reviewers and they did their best. However, most were already handling more than three hundred group lending clients. With no relief from their other responsibilities, there was a limit to what they could do. People applying for the new loans ended up waiting over a month, on average, for approval—a lag that proved more important than the interest rates that were the focus of the study.

FAILURE TO LEARN NEW AND DIFFERENT SKILLS

Partner organizations engaging in research almost always take on some changes to protocol, like having tellers provide the TFS savings promise prompt. But sometimes researchers end up asking people to do vastly different jobs than they are used to, and jobs for which they did not necessarily sign up. This raises the question of staff capacity and appetite to learn new skills and routines. In a case we will see in chapter 6, a Peruvian microfinance bank bundled financial literacy training, a service that could potentially help clients repay their loans (and which the clients wanted in any event), with their basic credit product. To minimize additional staff costs and time burden on clients, they appointed loan officers as the trainers and tasked them with delivering the curriculum during their weekly re-payment meetings over the course of a year. This seemed to be an efficient solution, until they discovered not all loan officers were great teachers.

Similarly, in chapter 11 we will discuss a case where an Indian microfinance giant partnered with an insurer to bundle basic health insurance policies with their loans. Again, loan officers were tapped to do the major legwork: describing and marketing the policies to borrowers, and helping people complete front-end paperwork like enrollment and claim forms. Again, their performance was disappointing. It turned out that many good loan officers made lousy insurance agents.

COMPETING PRIORITIES AND LACK OF BUY-IN

TFS and the cases just described, which we will discuss later, are just a few examples of a dishearteningly familiar story: partner organization leadership is enthusiastic about doing an evaluation; they work with researchers to zero in on a question that has both research and practical value; they co-design an intervention and experiment to answer it empirically; they assign and train staff, often with researchers' direct oversight; and then the wheels fall off in implementation. Where does the breakdown occur?

As researchers we understand the motivation for the study, see (and presumably care about) the potential benefits from completing it, and feel ownership and investment in the plan that we helped conceive. Perhaps the same is true of key leaders in the partner organization. But the research study is typically just one among many products, programs, or initiatives competing for the partner's attention. Indeed, a study itself might have competing priorities built right in. Suppose we are evaluating a brand-new product. As researchers, our interest is typically in exploring the data from a clean, well-executed test. If the product is a smash hit, we learn something; and if it is not, we learn something different. But partners (understandably) do not want to launch products that flop. If an opportunity arose to tweak a failing product, say, in a way that made it more appealing to customers but invalidated the experiment, what would they choose? Gathering rigorous evidence is valuable, both for the partner's operations and for the field in general; but is it more important than offering products and services people want? One hopes this tension does not arise, but if it does it can derail an evaluation. (Hint: the punchline in that scenario is to pilot!)

Such tensions arise at all levels, from the executive suite to the break room. What does a research study mean to a frontline employee—a bank teller in Mexico, a loan officer in Peru, or a nurse in rural Malawi? It's an additional assignment, often framed as a "special project" to help "these professors" (*cut to smiling, khaki-clad project team*) with "their research." It is not part of your core job description, and you probably did not volunteer for it. You are likely not receiving any additional compensation for helping. (Studies have confirmed the obvious: paying incentives to adhere to protocols does work! Although first-best is when adhering to the protocol actually helps employees do their jobs better.) You are asked to attend training sessions to learn all the new stuff you will be doing. At the same time, you are expected to keep doing your current job and you still answer to your supervisor—but now she is joined occasionally by a research assistant (who might be a few years younger than you and might be new in-country), who is suddenly giving you feedback on your work. If a conflict arises between your new and old responsibilities, as happened with the teller in the TFS study, you use your best judgment—likely after glancing over your shoulder to see if your supervisor or the research assistant is watching.

If this might be disconcerting for junior employees, how much more so for middle management? A study brings new routines to implement and new standards to enforce. Again, these are typically in addition to—not in place of—existing responsibilities, like hitting sales quotas or managing a lending portfolio. Perhaps (hopefully) senior leaders have explained or presented the rationale behind the research, but you did not have a role in shaping the question, nor were you consulted about the feasibility of implementation. And you likely will not have a say in how the findings are put into practice. The research assistant is almost certainly younger and less experienced than you and yet appears somehow to have the ear of upper management.

When researchers join forces with a partner and thus tap into its organizational structure, getting buy-in up and down the chain of command can be the difference between success and failure. This might mean institutionalizing the needs of the study in some concrete ways—incorporating study activities into staff performance reviews or providing incentives for staff to participate fully. Of course, this requires engaging with partner management at all levels. Consensus building is messy work, but it is essential.

HEADS IN THE SAND

Suppose all the consensus building and setup work have been done carefully. The partner is thoroughly engaged, the study launches successfully and runs smoothly, and data start rolling in. Of course, final results are not available until the study formally concludes, but in many cases the research team and partner have some preview of the outcome from either midline data or direct experience in the field.

Ideally, getting a glimpse of the finish line is motivating and encourages everyone to stay the course. But what if the likely answer is not what was hoped for or expected—say, if midline data suggest the intervention under study is having no impact? Partners may become discouraged and stop putting forth the effort necessary to see the project through. It is not uncommon in such cases for all kinds of unexpected practical issues to arise. Suddenly staff are no longer available to do project-related work, managers postpone or cancel meetings with researchers, and the like.

Disengagement might be a rational response to changing circumstances, from the partner's perspective: If we now know the answer (with some confidence), why continue tying up staff and resources in research? Endline surveys, audits, and other remaining steps crucial to the academic process may be less relevant to partners. They might prefer to work through the implications of the study's (likely) result on finances or operations, or simply try something new.

When midline data suggest a low- or no-impact result, partners may feel that the researchers have done them a disservice. This is especially likely if they went into evaluation with great confidence in the efficacy of their program (as many practitioners do). They likely hoped the research findings would endorse their work and raise their organization's stature; instead they face a result that may raise questions about their program. They might simply conclude the study was flawed rather than doubt their initial confidence. One hopes to talk partners through such difficult moments—and manage expectations from the outset—but they may be eager to wrap up the project and move on.

The overarching lesson here is to choose carefully. Seek out partners who genuinely want to learn about their programs and products; who are ready, willing, and able to dedicate an appropriate amount of organizational capacity to research; and who are open to the possibility that not all the answers will be rosy.

* * *

This advice does come with a caveat: Are organizations that genuinely want to learn representative of all organizations? To tackle this question, Hunt Allcott of New York University conducted a fascinating exercise with utilities in the United States (2015). The utility company Opower had developed a conservation program called Home Energy Reports: customized reports, mailed to utility customers, that compared their energy usage with that of their neighbors and offered conservation tips. Ten initial utilities tested the Opower program and, encouraged by the results, those utilities and 48 others decided to implement the program in 101 additional experiments. Allcott compared the results of the ten initial RCTs with those of the expansion and asked whether they were consistent. They were not. The impacts observed in the ten pilot sites were significantly greater than those in the expansion. The financial implications of this upward bias were considerable: using the ten initial pilot sites to predict the results of a nationwide scale-up overestimated actual energy savings by half a billion dollars.

Unwittingly, Opower had initially tested the program in relatively favorable settings that were not representative of the country as a whole. Allcott identified that this happened in three ways. First, utilities in the initial pilot targeted the program to households with the most room for improvement—those with high energy usage. Second, the utilities in the initial pilot were disproportionately in areas with environmentalist and high-income households—that is, areas more likely to be responsive to the program. Finally, for-profit utilities, which tend to experience lower efficacy when implementing such programs, were less likely to join the initial pilot.

The particular mechanisms in the Opower example are less important than the general result: beware of the selection process when choosing partners, and do not assume that results from a first study (or even a few replications) will easily generalize to a broader population of implementing organizations. This may not be a problem if the study is designed as a stand-alone—for example, as a proof-of-concept that a particular intervention works—but it is important when thinking about potential for scale. The organizations most eager to participate in research may be those with unusually high capacity, or farsighted leadership, or other characteristics that might make them more successful than the average implementer.

CHAPTER 4

SURVEY AND MEASUREMENT EXECUTION PROBLEMS

MANTRA: *Thou shalt collect data carefully.*

There is an old adage about the largely thankless task of housekeeping: it goes unnoticed unless it is done poorly. The same could be said of surveying and measurement in field research. At its best, data collection is like a clean window onto the world: transparent, the image beyond neither dimmed nor distorted. (As we saw in the chapter on technical design flaws, this is more an ideal than a real possibility.) Data collection aims to capture information with sufficient precision and accuracy to allow an unbiased test of hypotheses. The data are a means to an end.

A glance at a typical journal article confirms this. Theory is motivated and contextualized by reference to past research; equations are derived line by line; models are explicated. On the other hand, details about data collection methods and processes earn a brief reference, if any, in the experimental design section. The juiciest bits often end up as footnotes or online appendices—and sometimes not even that.

Something is amiss here. Theory does merit more discussion because it—as opposed to the mechanics of data collection—is often the novel, innovative component of the work being presented. But make no mistake: a field study that tests a theory is only as strong as its data. And, as any development field researcher will attest, collecting accurate and precise data is an enormous undertaking.

In the work we discuss in this book, and across much of the RCTs-for-development field, data come from one of three sources. First, and most common, surveyors meet with subjects—usually face to face but sometimes via phone or text message—and ask questions, recording responses as they go. Sometimes they also measure key health variables such as height and weight. Second, data from third parties can be used, such as voting records from the government, credit bureau reports, or rainfall data from weather stations. Finally, partner organizations' administrative records capture information like sales of health services, attendance at training sessions, or bank account balances, withdrawal and deposit dates, and amounts.

Collecting data from the first source, in-person surveying, is often the most time- and labor-intensive part of a field study. It is also a hotbed of failures, full of opportunities to misstep.

FAILURES OF SURVEYS THEMSELVES

Until recently, the vast majority of surveys in development field studies were done the old-fashioned way, on clipboards with pen and paper. It would not be unusual to conduct, say, a thirty-page survey with two thousand respondents. That meant keeping track of lots of paper. Reams and shelves and rooms full of paper. Paper that was susceptible to the elements. Paper that, while changing hands from surveyors to office staff to data entry personnel, had to stay meticulously ordered and bundled to avoid mixing surveys. In the limbo between surveying and data entry (when survey data are digitized), simple clerical failures could cripple a study.

If one managed to keep all the paper straight, the question of legibility remained. Surveys are often conducted in difficult settings: standing beside a produce seller in a busy market while she conducts her business; sitting in a rickety plastic chair under a leaky awning during a rainstorm. Handwriting suffers and ink smudges. Employing a team of scrutinizers, whose job is to check incoming surveys for consistency, completeness, and legibility—and to catch surveyor errors as soon as they arise— emerged as a best practice.

Amid these formidable (albeit pedestrian) challenges, the past five years have seen a huge shift from paper-and-pen surveying to electronic data collection using laptops, PDAs, or even smartphones to record answers from face-to-face surveys. This has several advantages but also poses risks. It requires electricity to charge devices, often a challenge in rural areas of developing countries. It also invites researchers to add layers of complexity onto the surveys themselves, which can be a Pandora's box.

* * *

One early use of laptops for this kind of surveying was in a study in South Africa that measured the impact of receiving a small loan (sort of like microcredit, although targeted to salaried individuals instead of microentrepreneurs). Researchers Lia Fernald and Rita Hamad of the University of California– Berkeley, Dean Karlan, and Jonathan Zinman of Dartmouth College wanted to know the impact of access to credit on mental health and planned to ask about both topics individually. But they were unsure about the order: In the survey, should they ask about respondents' past borrowing—and thus about repayment and default, which could potentially bring up stressful memories—before or after asking about mental health? They suspected that "priming" people with stressful memories might influence their answers to the mental health questions.

To investigate this hunch, they built in a mini test. They decided to randomize whether the mental health questions came before or after the past borrowing questions. Since the survey was computerized, this was (or, at least, seemed) as simple as adding a line of code to randomize the order in which the two sections were displayed.

Unfortunately, the survey software proved to be buggy. When the mental health section was supposed to appear second, instead it was skipped altogether. Nobody caught the error until it was too late: most surveys had already been conducted. So the researchers ended up posing mental health questions to only half of the respondents. For one, this meant they could not test their methodological hypothesis that the order of sections might influence responses. It also lowered the statistical power for the mental health component of the study, since they now had only half the data! On the upside, since it was a random half, analysis was still internally valid; and they did in fact find important, and statistically significant, results. But, had they retained the full sample size, the results likely would have been even more robust and given them a chance to dig deeper, examining heterogeneity, for example.

Simple lesson learned: complexity in the survey can be good, but be careful not to overdesign.

SURVEYORS MISBEHAVING

Even as laptops, tablets, PDAs, and other technologies are incorporated, surveying remains a very human process. Especially in settings where language, literacy levels, and familiarity with technology vary, research subjects rarely interact directly with machines. Instead, dedicated surveyors typically sit with respondents, read questions out loud, and record spoken answers as text.

As with technology versus paper and pen, this is decidedly a mixed blessing. On the upside: surveyors can adapt, interpret, and problem-solve when necessary. If a respondent does not comprehend a question, or if an answer suggests he misunderstood, the surveyor can go back and clarify. Surveyors can manage distractions, keeping respondents engaged—sometimes for hours—even as they handle occasional work or household duties. Effective surveyors also create rapport that encourages respondents to open up and share more than they might reveal otherwise.

On the downside: surveyors can adapt, interpret, and problem-solve *whenever they want*. Sometimes intentionally but often unwittingly, surveyors make subtle choices on the fly that can substantially impact respondents' answers—for instance, altering the wording of questions, prompting specific responses, or asking guiding questions. At best, these are honest (and random) mistakes made in pursuit of accurate data, but sometimes they are deliberate. Surveyors might suspect that certain answers will make respondents more likely to receive services or that certain answers will prompt additional questions and therefore more work. Indeed, many failures can be chalked up to a simple (and enormously frustrating) desire among some surveyors to avoid work. The following story is a case in point.

In the spring of 2013, researchers Pascaline Dupas of Stanford University, Dean Karlan, Jonathan Robinson of the University of California–Santa Cruz, and Diego Ubfal of Bocconi University were finishing up a study in Malawi on the impact of savings. With baseline and intervention already completed, six teams of six surveyors each were sent to the field to conduct the endline. Each surveyor was given a list of participants and instructed to take them through the final survey.

The endline was a long questionnaire—about three hours in total—with modules covering diverse topics from financial literacy to farming inputs. The researchers built in a variety of checks to the data collection process: team leaders accompanied their surveyors to the field and sat in on interviews; scrutinizers reviewed filled-in paper surveys for completeness, consistency, and legibility; and auditors randomly selected 10 percent of completed surveys to be reconducted as an accuracy check.

Rachel Levenson, the researcher running field operations, was conducting an audit re-survey when she noticed something strange. From where she sat with her respondent, she had a view of a neighboring household that was also part of the project. It happened that one of the surveyors—let's call him Surveyor X—had just arrived there to conduct the endline. While continuing her re-survey, she watched him sit down with his respondent, take out his survey notebook and pen, and start the interview. About forty-five minutes in he seemed to stop talking with the respondent altogether but continued to write in his notebook. After a while longer he packed up his things, shook the respondent's hand, and left—long before the expected three hours were up.

Rachel saw Surveyor X shortly after he had left the house and asked what had happened. He said that the respondent had needed to cut the survey short to visit a relative in the hospital, but he was confident there was no need to return: "Don't worry," he said. "We got all the information we need." Rachel gave him the benefit of the doubt for the moment. Later that day another supervisor saw Surveyor X sitting by himself on a bench in a bus depot in the town. He had his survey notebook open and was writing diligently. When the supervisor approached, Surveyor X quickly closed the notebook. He insisted he was "just checking" a survey he had completed earlier—a task with which the supervisor happily offered to help. But despite many requests, he refused to open his notebook and left in a huff.

Surveyor X's behavior suggested to Rachel he was doctoring his surveys somehow. They went back to many of his respondents and audited intensively to figure out the following: Had he asked all the questions he was supposed to? Had he recorded respondents' answers faithfully? The answer was a resounding and discouraging "no." Just 36 percent of Surveyor X's surveys had been completed satisfactorily. The rest had gaps: sometimes just a few questions, sometimes many. Compiling the results of their audit, it was clear that Surveyor X had been routinely skipping over parts of the survey during his interviews with respondents and covering it up by inventing responses after the fact.

This meant the research team had to make some costly detours: rechecking Surveyor X's work top to bottom; salvaging surveys where possible by reconducting specific modules or, in some cases, the entire three-hour interview; and discarding data in the few cases where re-surveying was not possible. Parting ways with Surveyor X was itself a trying experience. When the researchers confronted him with the results of their investigation and fired him, he flatly denied any wrongdoing, accused them of a laundry list of misdeeds, and threatened to sue. (Further investigations found no truth in his allegations, and he never filed a lawsuit.) Following his dismissal, the research team paused field activities to bring the entire survey team together for a daylong audit and training session, reemphasizing the importance of following the survey from start to finish and taking the time to ask every question.

Lessons learned: Build a robust process for continuous monitoring and auditing. On top of that process, *always* keep your eyes open. If something seems fishy, investigate—quickly—before making accusations. When you are confident you have found a problem, nip it in the bud. And let the team know you are aware of, and responsive to, what is going on in the field.

INABILITY TO KEEP TRACK OF RESPONDENTS

Even when surveyors carry out their responsibilities faithfully, success is hardly assured. Respondents often present obstacles of their own.

Simply keeping track of research subjects' identities over time is a pervasive challenge. This is rarely the case in developed countries, where reliable and widely held personal IDs like social security numbers and driver's licenses are the norm. But researchers working in developing countries often have much less to go on. Suppose you are studying a seasonal agriculture intervention with a full year between baseline and endline. At baseline you likely collect a first and last name (note that spelling can vary widely),[1] some personal information (e.g., age, how much school they completed), and some characteristics of the household (e.g., where it is located, who lives there, what kind of crops they grow). Come endline, will that be enough to ensure you are talking to the same person you interviewed a year earlier? Again, there is room for both honest mistakes and intentional gaming.

We will see the latter play out in chapter 8, where we discuss a test of a youth savings program in Uganda. Some of the survey modules, designed to elicit preferences, required respondents to play live games with small amounts of cash ($1–2), supplied by the researchers. They were simply following best practice: it is widely believed[2] that playing with even a nominal amount of real money produces more accurate data than asking hypothetical questions about imaginary sums. However, the cash ultimately did more harm than good. Once word about the compensation got out, other young people who were not included in the survey began impersonating respondents, hoping to dupe their way into a couple dollars.

PROBLEMS WITH MEASUREMENT TOOLS

As mentioned earlier, surveys are the most common method for collecting data in the field, but they are not the only one. Hoping to avoid the very kinds of failures just discussed, researchers sometimes prefer to use measurement tools that capture data directly, without asking questions. The potential of such tools is compelling: they promise to cut out many of the messy, human steps that make it so difficult to get precise and accurate data. How much better, for instance, to have people stand on a scale than to ask them their weight verbally?

The problem with measurement tools is that they do not always work as advertised. To use the same example, scales can be miscalibrated. And, as a general rule, the more complex the tool, the more ways it can fail.

* * *

Researchers Suresh de Mel of the University of Peradeniya, Dhammika Herath of the University of Gothenburg, and David McKenzie and Yuvraj Pathak of the World Bank were preparing to conduct a study on Sri Lankan microenterprises. Part of their research plan involved regularly compiling the inventories of small retail businesses as a way to measure sales (and, eventually, profits). Since most businesses in their sample stocked dozens of different products and did very little formal record keeping, it appeared that tracking inventory would involve a lot of counting by hand. A typical approach would be to send research assistants to each business, say, once a week, and have them physically verify the inventory piece by piece.

The researchers considered an alternative approach: radio frequency identification (RFID) tagging. Using this technology, each individual product (e.g., one bar of soap) could be tagged with a small sticker that contained a scannable chip. Unlike a barcode, which needs to be visible to be read, RFID tags can be scanned from a few feet away and without a direct line of sight. As such, inventorying could in theory be done without the cumbersome process of capturing each item individually. Instead, research assistants could simply arrive at the business, aim their scanners at the shelves, and capture all the data instantly.

Before deciding on RFID technology for the whole study, the researchers wisely ran a pilot. They chose twenty microenterprises typical of their sample and tried tagging and scanning their inventories. As expected in a pilot, they discovered their share of operational kinks: the printer that created the RFID tags was heavy and impractical to transport from business to business; the scanning took about thirty minutes per business, far longer than anticipated; and the tags, at $0.22 each, were costly relative to the goods being sold (e.g., individual bars of soap).

Time and cost notwithstanding, the big question was accuracy. Did RFID produce more reliable inventory figures than other methods? To answer this, the researchers compared the RFID scans with two additional ways of capturing inventory levels: first, counting by hand (this was considered the "gold standard" of accuracy); and second, asking the business owners with a survey. In a word, the answer was "no." Across the pilot, the scanners successfully counted only 25 percent of products. There were some lessons about specific items—shoes scanned easily; fresh fruit was a disaster—but the results were mixed and disappointing overall. Scanners' effectiveness also varied considerably from day to day and from shop to shop.

By comparison, old-fashioned surveying proved a great way to measure inventory levels. On average, business owners' estimates were 99 percent of the hand-counted totals. Perhaps even more impressive was their precision: taken item by item, half of all their survey responses were between 91 and 104 percent of the hand-counted totals. The simple questionnaires beat the high-tech approach hands down—and, not surprisingly, the researchers decided against using RFID tags in the full study.

CHAPTER 5

LOW PARTICIPATION RATES

MANTRA: *Thou shalt reduce the implementer's predicted participation rates by half, or maybe even more.*

We consider ourselves optimists, but two lessons we have learned are that things rarely go as well as advocates predict they will and that Rumsfeldian "unknown unknowns" typically lead to less, not more, success. These lessons have a simple implication for running randomized trials: participation rates (the portion of eligible or targeted individuals who actually avail themselves of the program being tested, also called "take-up") will likely be lower than expected. Low participation rates squeeze the effective sample size for a test, making it more difficult, statistically, to identify a positive treatment effect. There are two moments in which low participation rates can materialize: during the intake process to a study or intervention, or after random assignment to treatment or control.

LOW PARTICIPATION DURING INTAKE

Low participation during the intake process often occurs when marketing a program to the general public. The research plan might be to offer the program widely and then to randomly assign to treatment or control those who voluntarily come forward to participate. But perhaps far fewer people come forward than anticipated. Or perhaps many come forward, but most of those people do not meet the organization's requirements for participation. Either way, researchers are left with fewer research subjects than they need.

* * *

This happened in 2009 when researchers Sebastian Galiani and Martin Rossi of the Universidad de San Andrés partnered with LIFIA, a local information technology research lab, to evaluate its new training program for postsecondary learners. As RCTs go, it was a simple setup. The researchers told LIFIA they would need to find 90 willing and able students, and randomly assign half to receive the training and the other half not. "Willing and able" in this case boiled down to a few criteria. To be included in the study, participants had to: (1) be age 17–24; (2) live within commuting distance of Universidad de La Plata, where the trainings were to be held; (3) have graduated from secondary school or be in their final year of it; (4) not be enrolled in any tertiary institution; and (5) pass a qualification exam to show they could handle the course material.

An open call, posted on and around the campus of Universidad de La Plata, invited people to the qualification exam and briefly explained the training curriculum and the other criteria for inclusion. The plan was to conduct and score the exam, tap 90 of those passing (choosing randomly among all passers if there were more than 90) to be participants, and then deliver the training sessions over four months beginning in August, contemporaneous with the school year.

When over 90 people came to sit for the test, the researchers were pleased. Less so when the results came back: only a small portion had scored well enough to qualify. Undeterred, they put up more flyers and scheduled a second test date. Again they were pleased when the exam room filled up; and again they were disappointed when the results declared they still had not hit their 90-person target. They managed to squeeze in a third date before the start of the school year but came up short yet again.

With fewer than 90 participants, the study would have been underpowered—likely unable to detect effects of the magnitude the researchers expected to see. Going ahead with the smaller sample would have required convincing themselves that the training could plausibly have a much larger impact than they had initially thought. They saw no reason to change their expectations and so abandoned the study.

* * *

The same challenge is familiar to social science laboratory researchers at universities the world over, but they have a key advantage. When they post flyers around campus advertising an experiment and do not get enough volunteers, they have some simple solutions: Double down on advertising by posting more flyers! Take an extra week or two to get more participants. Maybe increase the compensation promised, to entice more people.

Researchers working in the field with partner organizations often face inflexible constraints in trying to cope with low participation during intake. Maybe the program or service being tested belongs not to the researchers but to a partner firm, who cannot simply "make it more enticing," as that would be unprofitable. Maybe the cost of increased compensation for participants would be prohibitive. Maybe there is a programmatic reason why the eligibility criteria cannot be broadened to accept more people. In Argentina, for instance, perhaps the qualification exam was difficult because the training itself was difficult, in which case lowering the threshold score would have served only to draw in underqualified students likely to fail. Sometimes these issues can be addressed, sometimes not.

LOW PARTICIPATION AFTER RANDOM ASSIGNMENT

The second type of low participation—that which occurs after subjects have been randomly assigned to treatment or control—is a more daunting problem and is less likely solvable than low participation at the intake phase. Here, a sample frame was already identified. Treatment and control groups were established. Maybe a baseline survey was even carried out. The program and evaluation are proceeding. And all of this was done with an unfortunately optimistic prediction that more would participate than ultimately did.

Here is a typical scenario. Researchers partner with a microlender to study how credit changes entire communities over time: Do people in the community begin doing different kinds of work? Are their earnings different than before? To design the experiment, the researchers work with the microlender to estimate as best they can (1) what portion of residents, on average, would actually take loans if they were available; and (2) how big an effect those loans would have on the outcomes they cared about (earnings, for example). Based on these estimates, they calculate an appropriate sample size, say, 250 communities. Next they randomly choose, from a list of 250 eligible villages, 125 to enter in the next two years (treatment group); and they commit to stay away from the remainder (the control group). The lender then does its job by entering the treatment villages and actively marketing loans, and by staying out of the control villages. But, in the treatment villages, fewer people come in and borrow than they had originally estimated.

Across all 250 villages there are indeed many borrowers (in treatment villages) and many non-borrowers (in *both* treatment and control villages), but one cannot make direct comparisons between them. Doing so would undermine the entire randomized trial by introducing selection biases—because borrowing is a choice, and those who *chose* to borrow could be materially different from those who *chose* not to borrow. In any event, individual-level comparisons may be beside the point, as such programs often claim to have impacts at the community level. Thus the researchers are locked into their village-level study design, comparing entire treatment villages to entire control villages. From this vantage, non-borrowers simply dilute the impact of treatment. (Presumably they are more likely to observe sweeping transformation in a village if, say, 80 percent of eligible residents take loans than if just 20 percent do.) Less concentrated treatment requires a larger sample, all else being equal. And this late in the game, after the program has been rolled out and a baseline survey done, expanding the sample is a complicated proposition. It is not impossible, but resources must be available (more surveys!), the organization has to be willing and able to go out and find more eligible villages, the timeline must be sufficiently flexible to allow for a pause while new villages are added, and so forth.

Sometimes plenty of people sign up for the program being tested and the research still fails: low participation can arise during program delivery as implementers wrestle with new activities and routines. In chapter 7, we will see a microfinance bank in Ghana that launched a new loan product in connection with a study. Initial client demand was in line with estimates the researchers had used in necessary sample size calculations. But despite a healthy number of applications, bottlenecks in the review process proved disastrous. Many clients withdrew their loan requests in frustration before receiving a decision. Ultimately the bank made very few loans—nowhere near enough to do meaningful analysis.

One final point: wherever in the research process it occurs, low participation among those targeted for treatment potentially implies low impact. If very few of those targeted receive the program or service, then you do not need fancy research and surveys to know it did not make a difference for intended recipients on the whole. As in the case of loan application bottlenecks just mentioned, maybe the core idea is still viable but implementation was lacking. Or maybe the idea was genuinely bad. Either way, no delivery means no impact.

OVERCONFIDENCE AND CREDULOUSNESS

Why does this happen? Why do implementing partner organizations consistently overestimate the level of demand for their services? Surely those running their own programs should be better at predicting participation rates than outsiders. Yet this is our experience as researchers.

Behavioral psychology has something to say about this. People tend to be optimistic about things they control— actually, more to the point, about things they *perceive* they control. As researchers we often have a say in the design of intervention being tested and the way it is delivered; now it seems as simple as rolling it out and watching the people flock to it. (We often discount the vast array of external factors that need to coalesce for this to happen.) Such optimism, a known cognitive bias,[1] makes us routinely overestimate the likelihood of participation in something we want people to do.

At the same time, another cognitive bias makes us routinely *underestimate* the likelihood of nonparticipation: we rarely take the time to think explicitly about the many, varied, and endlessly surprising ways our plans could go awry (this book notwithstanding). Instead, we tend to tacitly lump them all together in a single mental bucket, which we usually try not to think about too much. But as it turns out, the very fact of not sorting through and considering the individual elements in this bucket makes us weigh these factors too lightly when judging probabilities.

This phenomenon was described and characterized by Amos Tversky and Derek Koehler (1994) and was demonstrated in a classic experiment by other researchers,[2] who asked subjects how much they would be willing to pay for a hypothetical insurance policy. To some, they described a policy that covered hospitalization for any disease or accident. To others, they described a policy that covered hospitalization for any reason at all. Now, clearly the latter policy is more valuable—it covers everything the former does and more. But, believe it or not, the former fetched a higher (hypothetical) price! Simply naming disease and accident as possible reasons for hospitalization sets off a cascade of associated examples, thoughts, and memories—all of which conspire to make us feel like diseases and accidents happen all the time. As a result, we implicitly assign a higher likelihood to these events (and thus to the need for hospitalization) and offer a higher price for the insurance policy. By contrast, the vague "any reason at all" conjures up no salient examples and results in a lower offer. If we made a habit of explicitly listing the reasons why people might not participate in our program or use our product, we would likely come to more conservative—and more accurate—estimates of take-up rates.

In a case we will see in chapter 11, a microfinance bank in India began bundling a health insurance policy with its loans. The bank's leadership understood that providing insurance along with credit made a lot of sense: it could achieve broad distribution by leveraging their extensive client network, and it helped mitigate the possibility that borrowers would default as a result of health problems. There was also an element of genuine social value: this would bring actuarially fairly priced health coverage to thousands of uninsured people. Presuming most clients would accept it, they decided to make the policy a mandatory addition to their loans. They were sorely mistaken. Clients, it turned out, had *many* reasons to balk: they did not like the policy itself, they could not bear the additional cost, or they simply resented being forced to buy insurance.

Lessons like this have taught us to always ask implementing partners for data to back up estimates about participation and not to rely on perception. Even with data in hand, we have learned to dig deep and question our assumptions. Will everyone who shows up to the first meeting follow through and attend the others? What portion of people who say they would like a loan will actually take one? Sometimes one can find data from analogous projects and settings to guess at the right answer, while other times one might investigate directly by running a pre-pilot; the point is to make an informed estimate. Beware the notion that "if we build it, they will come." Experience suggests a bit of healthy skepticism at the outset is a good thing.

PART II

CASE STUDIES

CHAPTER 6

CREDIT AND FINANCIAL LITERACY TRAINING

No Delivery Means No Impact

BACKGROUND + MOTIVATION

Microcredit institutions often do more than merely make loans. Many aim to go above and beyond, to help clients learn entrepreneurial skills or improve their health. Even for-profit lenders may do this strictly for profit reasons, if they believe it will improve loan repayment rates and create more loyal customers. This additional support from lenders can take many different forms, from social contracts where borrowers commit to positive behaviors like keeping their kids in school to financial education courses teaching about credit and savings, budgeting, business planning, and the like.

The evidence suggests that such supplemental training programs work sometimes, but not always. For instance, a study with a microlender in Peru[1] found that borrowers who received business training increased their knowledge and were more likely to become repeat customers. On the other hand, a study in Mexico[2] found that an award-winning financial literacy program was met with little demand and had low impact among marginal participants.[3]

Maybe the mixed results are due to the wide variety of programs out there. Training courses vary on every dimension imaginable: content, delivery channels, length, integration with other services, charisma of the instructor conducting the training, and more. A host of questions remain. Some are operational: Who should deliver the training; when and where? In practice, microcredit institutions often take an in-house approach, piggybacking on existing infrastructure—operations in rural and remote areas, loan officers who know clients personally, a regular schedule of face-to-face meetings—to provide services directly. Is this ideal? Other questions concern the training itself: What topics should be covered? What are the best ways—media, exercises, and so forth—to deliver financial education? On these issues there are common practices and hunches but far less systematic evidence about what works best.

The growth of remote learning platforms like Khan Academy and MOOCs suggests a compelling way to provide additional support at scale, especially in settings with limited traditional educational infrastructure like the rural areas of developing countries where many microfinance institutions operate. Could such an approach, using multimedia technology to deliver high-quality lessons, drive learning and better outcomes for clients? There is healthy debate[4] on technology's potential and proper role as a development tool. Some proponents argue that, at scale, it can change the game—that giving every child on Earth a laptop would dramatically transform learning and education. Critics counter that technology is not an answer in itself: it might amplify or accelerate progress, but it can never replace the ingenuity and effort of a human teacher. As empiricists we do not have a principled position on this question; our approach is simply to identify such debates and set up appropriate tests.[5] By evaluating programs that employ technology, we can learn whether—and under what circumstances—it works to alleviate poverty.

STUDY DESIGN

In 2009, researchers Alberto Chong of the InterAmerican Development Bank (now at the University of Ottawa), Dean Karlan, and Martin Valdivia of GRADE-Peru partnered with the Peruvian microfinance institution Arariwa to explore a number of these questions by implementing and testing a multimedia financial education program for clients.

The program was a nine-part curriculum based on materials created by international development nonprofit Freedom from Hunger and adapted to incorporate a variety of media and teaching techniques. At its heart were nine in-person training sessions, to be delivered by loan officers equipped with formal scripts and poster-style visual aids. Each session was supplemented by a five- to seven-minute DVD-based video module to be shown during the lecture; a twenty-five-minute radio program to reinforce the in-person and video content with testimonials; and a written homework assignment to encourage learners to reflect and commit to relevant behavior changes.

The researchers designed an RCT to test the training program in the field with borrowers. Of Arariwa's roughly 1,200 "communal banks"—that is, self-organized groups of 10–30 clients who took loans together—they selected 666 to participate (perhaps this oddly symbolic numerical choice is what doomed the study?). To ensure they could carry out the multimedia portions of the training, they included only groups with regular access to electricity and within broadcast range of radio stations. The design was simple: half the groups would be assigned to treatment and the other half to control. Groups assigned to treatment would receive in-person trainings with video supplements and would be instructed to complete the written homework assignments and listen to the radio supplements. Groups assigned to control would receive "placebo" in-person trainings about health and self-esteem that had no homework, video, or radio supplements.

As they were interested in studying the impact of financial literacy education on both financial knowledge and real-world financial choices, the researchers planned to collect two kinds of data. First, they would observe clients' actual repayment and savings behavior from Arariwa's administrative records. Second, they would conduct surveys of participants to learn about their household expenditures, financial literacy skills, and attitudes toward financial management.

IMPLEMENTATION PLAN

Spanning four types of media, scores of loan officers, thousands of clients, and much of the country of Peru, delivery of the trainings promised to be a complex undertaking. In a study just a year prior, with a different Peruvian microlender, the same researchers had successfully piggybacked trainings onto existing group meetings where borrowers met with their loan officers in person to make loan payments.[6] They decided to take the same approach with Arariwa and deliver the financial literacy program during regularly scheduled monthly group meetings.

In these meetings, which lasted about two hours, loan officers would take roughly forty minutes to deliver the scripted lesson and another five to seven minutes to show the video supplement on a TV or portable DVD player. (Depending on the group, meetings might be held in a bank branch, a community center, or a client's home or business. A working video setup was hardly guaranteed in these venues. In discussions before launch, most loan officers expressed confidence that they could access audio/video equipment for the trainings by borrowing from clients. Consequently, Arariwa purchased a few portable DVD players for the study, but not enough for every loan officer.)

Radio programming and written homework, the other two components of the training program, were delivered between the monthly meetings. The radio programs lasted twenty-five minutes each and were broadcast four times per month on local radio stations during off-peak hours. There were two reasons for this choice. First, off-peak airtime was cheaper, which helped control the cost of the study. Second, and more important, they wanted the broadcasts somewhat "out of the way" to help ensure treatment went just to those assigned and not to everybody. Radio was sufficiently popular among Arariwa's clients that primetime broadcasts likely would have been heard by many participants assigned to control, creating a spillover that would dilute the power of the study.

The written homework assignments, also to be completed between monthly meetings, were the last piece of the puzzle. They had two parts: first, a series of questions to verify that clients had listened to the radio program; and second, an exercise with written questions that prompted clients to sit with their families, discuss specific financial matters, and commit to behavior change in those areas. At the beginning of the study, clients in the treatment group were each given a workbook with all the homework assignments and space to write in their answers.

As they worked to supply all this content, Arariwa and the researchers considered the demand side, too: How could they encourage clients to actively participate? Rolling the in-person and video trainings into monthly repayment meetings made sense because clients were already required to attend. To give the radio and written components a boost, they decided to offer an additional incentive: at the beginning of each meeting the loan officer would check homework and give a prize to a client who had completed the assignment. If multiple clients had completed it, a winner was chosen by lottery.

Finally, there was the question of timing. Because a typical loan cycle lasted about four months, the researchers allotted eleven months for groups to complete the series of nine trainings. This allowed for two cycle-changeover meetings, where no training was done and groups could instead focus on closing the books on completed loans and initiating new ones. Within the eleven-month time frame, loan officers were allowed to schedule the trainings as they saw fit.

WHAT WENT WRONG IN THE FIELD + CONSEQUENCES

As it turned out, the loan officers did not do much training at all. A dismal 1 percent of groups assigned to treatment managed to complete the full training program in the time allotted. Most did not even come close: in the median group assigned to treatment, the loan officer delivered just three of the nine in-person sessions.

There were three big reasons why so little training was actually delivered. First, attendance at meetings was a problem. Some clients consistently arrived late and wanted to leave early. Others did not show up at all and instead sent their payments with other group members. Loan officers facing a poorly attended meeting often chose to postpone training in the hopes that attendance would be better next time. (It usually was not.) No doubt this was partly bad luck, but anecdotes from the field suggest that some clients missed meetings precisely to avoid the trainings. A few even asked their loan officers point-blank to discontinue the financial literacy program and "stop wasting our time."

Client delinquency was the second reason so few groups completed the training program. In an unlucky turn of events, Arariwa's loan officers faced unusually high delinquency rates during the study. Some areas had suffered severe flooding, interrupting livelihoods and hampering many clients' ability to repay. A loan officer's first responsibility was to collect payments; and when it came down to a choice between using limited meeting time to give a financial literacy lecture or using the time to track down a client (or many) late on payments, they usually chose the latter.

The third reason trainings did not happen was that loan officers simply chose not to do them. Some felt uncomfortable teaching—and reasonably so, as they had been given little training themselves on the material. Others felt it was not their job. They had been hired to help lend and collect money, not teach. For loan officers like these, trainings were a distraction and a burden. It is no surprise they found other activities to conduct during their monthly meetings.

Having so few clients complete the in-person trainings—the backbone of the intervention—effectively killed the study. After all, given that almost nobody received the training, there was no need to compare the outcomes of a mostly untreated treatment group to an untreated control group. As we saw briefly in the chapter on participation rates, many programs do not have perfect compliance. But the compliance rate here was particularly low (less than 1 percent of those assigned to treatment completed the training). Even if this 1 percent did generate a positive treatment effect, the study's sample was not large enough to detect it.

If the in-person trainings proved difficult to carry out, the multimedia supplements were nearly impossible, hampered by both a dearth of equipment and technical difficulties. Contrary to what they had said during pre-study planning, loan officers were often unable to borrow TVs and DVD players from clients, friends, or family. Radio segments were a bust because clients had a hard time tuning in. Some worked during the "off-peak" hours Arariwa had purchased for broadcast. Though researchers had targeted borrowing groups that had radio coverage, some clients lived in remote locations and could not listen to the radio at home. Finally, a few genuinely did not know how to tune their radios to a new station to hear the broadcasts.

Researchers interviewing loan officers after the study found that the video and radio components of the program reached even fewer clients than did the in-person sessions. By the numbers: the median group had seen only one video supplement (more than four in ten had not seen any); and less than 7 percent of clients listened regularly to the radio segments. Overall, among groups that completed at least one training session, only about one in five received the multimedia supplements as intended—a level of compliance so low that the study cannot even be said to have tested them.

WHAT WAS THE FAILURE?

In this case we see two major areas of failures: *research setting* and *partner organization challenges*.

There were a few distinct instances of the former. First, the field sites presented challenges to the use of technology. Despite (perhaps superficial) efforts in advance to assess the feasibility of delivering the intervention, implementation suffered from lack of audio/video equipment and from some clients' inconsistent access to radio. Second, the intervention itself was deceptively complex. The training may have seemed simple, but in reality there were many operational steps—in-person meetings, TV, DVD, radio broadcasts, and more—that all had to function well but did not. Given that it had not been piloted prior to the study, perhaps it was *not mature enough* for a randomized trial. Finally, there was an element of *bad timing* in the flooding that caused repayment problems for some clients, thus adding stress to loan officers' already full plates.

Indeed, *competing priorities* were a key partner organization challenge in this case. Loan officers were expected to deliver trainings without any lapses in, or relief from, their basic duties. When faced with a direct trade-off between their chief mandate—to make loans and collect payments on time—and an experimental add-on that most of their clients simply tolerated and some openly disliked, it is no surprise that financial education came in a distant second. Likely contributing to this challenge is the fact that lecturing about financial literacy (or any subject!) was a *new and unfamiliar task* for most loan officers, quite different from what they had been hired and trained to do.

LESSONS LEARNED + REMEDIATION

The first operational takeaway is to do more pre-testing. With the benefit of hindsight, two features of the intervention under study make it a strong candidate for a pilot. First, demand for financial education was unknown and operationally important. If clients really did not want it, they could potentially derail the study (e.g., by refusing to attend trainings, as some did) or could simply take their business elsewhere. Second, successful delivery of the intervention depended on a long chain of actions and conditions: borrowing of video equipment by loan officers, reliable power at group meeting sites, timely broadcasts by local radio stations, working radios in clients' homes, and much more. How many of these were beyond experimenters' direct control or occurred outside their view altogether? Pre-testing can reveal weak links in such chains.

A second operational lesson is about ongoing monitoring. This study did not fail all at once; it happened gradually—and there may have been opportunities to course-correct. Suppose the researchers had been able to see, at the three-month mark, that only a few groups had completed even a single training session. They might have responded by increasing the amount of time groups had to complete the program or hiring dedicated financial trainers to assist loan officers. Had they been aware of the abysmal take-up of the multimedia supplements, they could have purchased more portable DVD players. Changing protocols and parameters of a live study is typically a last resort, but it might be better than the alternative. As researchers we often face the reality of limited resources for data collection, and a common strategy is to concentrate funds into robust surveys at the baseline, endline, or both. This is a perfect example where investment in more monitoring data along the way could have been worthwhile.

Beyond generic operational lessons, this case offers two takeaways specific to financial literacy education. First, integrating technology is more of a hurdle than the researchers had initially thought, and future efforts will likely require a bigger investment to lay the groundwork for success. Not only must the educational content be high quality, but there are prerequisites, too: well-trained and charismatic trainers, functional equipment, power, and reasonably tech-savvy users, to name a few. The potential benefits of using video and radio recordings are evident (scalability, for one). But implementation is where the rubber meets the road—and in rural Peru, that road is made of dirt, pitted with holes, and lacking reliable streetlights. Individuals' access to technology is hardly guaranteed, let alone the existence of the underlying infrastructure (e.g., a reliable power grid) required to make it work.

Second, using credit staff from microfinance institutions to teach financial literacy is a complicated (but doable) proposition. Again, the upside is big and compelling: they already have access to hard-to-reach people; delivering financial education along with financial products and services makes intuitive sense; and there could be benefits to giving people relevant knowledge "just-in-time" to put it to use. But teaching is a specialized skill and requires intention, patience, and effort to do well. Given that not all loan officers will make good financial literacy instructors, is the best approach simply to train all the credit officers in hopes that most turn out alright? Or is a collaborative model better, where "trainers" train and credit officers just handle the loan procedures? These are important operational questions that would benefit from further research.

CHAPTER 7

INTEREST RATE SENSITIVITY

Ignoring the Elephant in the Room

BACKGROUND + MOTIVATION

Microloans enjoy a privileged reputation among household credit products. If you asked a typical person to describe them, you would likely get an answer about small, low-cost loans to the poor (often women) to help them build microenterprises and work their way out of poverty. This would be partly right. In fact, microloans come in a vast array of shapes, sizes, and flavors. Interest rates in particular vary tremendously, from under 20 percent APR (better than most credit cards) to well over 100 percent APR (which would violate usury laws in many states and countries but might still be better than the next best alternative, which for the poor is often an informal moneylender).

To some extent, the wide range of interest rates reflects an equally wide range of underlying variables—default rates, loan sizes, and staff-to-client ratios, just to name a few—that impact the cost of providing loans. But the reality is that few if any microfinance institutions determine their rates mechanically according to such factors. For most, setting interest rates is an exercise in heuristics. The process is often grounded in nearby examples and reference points: What are our competitors charging? What have we charged in the past? What restrictions, if any, does the government impose on the rates we can charge?

Microlenders could take a more calculated approach—by thinking of revenue as a function of interest rate and trying to maximize profits. Doing so would raise a new set of questions about the connection between interest rates and revenues. To understand that relationship, lenders would need to know, for a variety of interest rates: How many people will actually take loans? How large will those loans be? Will the default rate change as the interest rate changes? How will our costs change as the number of borrowers changes?

Answering such questions and setting rates accordingly could make for a better bottom line; it might also have impacts beyond profitability. For example, one could imagine different interest rates attracting different types of clients. For example, high rates might drive away all but the neediest, most cash-strapped borrowers.

Opportunity International Savings and Loans, Ltd. (OISL), one of Ghana's largest microfinance institutions, was interested in the implications of interest rate for both revenue and outreach. In 2006, they partnered with Dean Karlan, Chris Udry of Yale University, and Jonathan Zinman of Dartmouth College to test both questions with a randomized trial. This study has a special place in Dean's and Jacob's hearts, as it is how they first met. The project did not go so well, as you will now learn, but the collaboration and friendship were born.

STUDY DESIGN

The basic concept was simple: market loans to different people using a range of interest rates and observe how many and what kinds of people respond to the offer. In a setting like the United States, such a trial could be conducted easily using email or direct mail to market the loans, with credit scores as a proxy for financial information about borrowers. (In fact, banks run experiments like this all the time. You have likely been part of one if you have ever received a letter offering you a credit card.)

In Ghana, the setup was more complicated. Credit scores were nonexistent and most people did not have mailing or email addresses—especially OISL's potential customer base of mostly poor and lower-middle-class microentrepreneurs. Lack of this key infrastructure called for a face-to-face approach. A short six-question survey would be used to estimate poverty levels. Marketing would be done in person, with field staff visiting potential clients at their businesses, conducting the survey, presenting a promotional flyer, and briefly describing the loan offer.

One consequence of door-to-door marketing was sensitivity around local variation in interest rates: OISL did not want to be perceived as unfair, offering one rate to one person and a different rate to a neighbor. To minimize reputational risk, the researchers settled on a "clustered" design that treated entire micro-neighborhoods as single entities, assigning a single interest rate throughout. Clusters were defined according to natural boundaries—for example, a single row of stalls in a market or one block of a city street.

The research team identified 180 such clusters comprising 3,824 microentrepreneurs, spread across 12 busy commercial areas of the capital city of Accra, covering the services areas of three OISL branches. They randomly assigned each cluster to one of four interest rates: 24, 31, 38 (OISL's normal rate), or 45 percent.

The promotional flyers given to each business owner included the interest rate along with some marketing variations that were also part of the experiment: half the flyers displayed the interest rate as a flat annual percentage, the other half as a sample monthly loan payment; half featured a picture of a well-dressed bank employee, the other half a produce seller who looked like a typical OISL client; half said "Loans up to $1,500!" the other half "Loans up to $5,000!" Unlike the interest rates themselves, these marketing variations were randomized at the individual level.

Beneath the interest rate and marketing variations, the product was a personal loan for microentrepreneurs—a new offering for OISL. (Up to that point they had made only joint-liability loans, where clients borrowed in groups whose members cross-guaranteed for each other's debt.) For the new personal loan, applicants would need to name a guarantor whose income was sufficient to cover the debt and who committed to pay if the applicant defaulted. To further establish creditworthiness, applicants would provide information about their business assets and revenues, which would later be verified by a visit from a loan officer. Applicants could request loans with maturities from three to twelve months and were expected to use the money to expand or improve their businesses. (As a side note, what this means exactly is open to much debate in the microcredit space: some lenders demand actual receipts, some say merely that they expect borrowers to spend money on enterprise; others neither say nor expect anything and let borrowers do as they wish. The evidence is light on whether this matters at all in terms of changing investment behavior.)

Although actual borrowing was the main outcome of interest in the study, the research team designed software to track participants through the entire application process. Bank staff could log each successive step clients took: receiving the promotional offer in the field, visiting an OISL branch to inquire, initiating a loan application, completing the application (including providing a guarantor), and finally disbursement. On the back end, the brief surveys administered in the field were linked to these records to create a complete picture of individuals' poverty levels, the loan offers they had received, and how far they had gone in the application process.

IMPLEMENTATION PLAN

It was decided that OISL credit officers, already familiar with the loan application and administration process, would staff the study. In the first stage of the project they served primarily as marketers, making drop-in sales calls to each of the more than 3,800 business owners that had been identified in advance. (They were instructed to be persistent, making up to three return visits if the owner was unavailable when they arrived.) When they met the owners, they went through a set of roughly scripted talking points: introducing themselves and OISL, presenting the promotional flyer (which included the interest rate as well as the other marketing variations), administering the short poverty-level survey, and inviting them to visit the local OISL branch if they wanted to inquire about the offer.

As marketing continued cluster by cluster over the course of about four months, loan officers rotated between the field and the branch, where they received incoming customers responding to the loan offers. When business owners came in with the promotional flyers they had received in the field, they were directed to a desk in the lobby where the loan officer on duty registered their names in the study database (which called up information collected during the field visit), answered any questions they had, and helped them start an application if they were interested.

Between door-to-door sales, special offers, and database software, the study added new routines to a variety of bank operations. To identify possible hiccups, OISL and the researchers conducted a limited pilot in one branch prior to launch. Consistent with its implementation focus, the pilot ran just long enough to test the marketing and in-branch routines—not long enough to observe people as they made their way through the loan application process. Even seeing business owners' initial responses to the loan offer was a benefit, though, as it provided a rough estimate of the take-up rate that researchers could expect in the full study. What they observed—just over 10 percent of business owners coming into the branch in response to the offer—corroborated the initial estimates the researchers had used to calculate sample size for the study, so they proceeded to launch.

WHAT WENT WRONG IN THE FIELD + CONSEQUENCES

In some ways the study was successful: marketing in the field and handling of inquiries at the branches ran generally without incident. Business owners' responses to the loan offers were also in line with expectations. Overall, about 15 percent came into a branch to inquire—even more than had done so in the pilot. Trouble arose not amid the intricacies of study protocols but in the loan application process, which proved far more onerous and cumbersome than expected.

The single biggest hang-up was the guarantor requirement. Most applicants had a hard time finding family or friends who could commit to cover a loan of, say, $2,000. Either they did not know anyone in such a position, or they felt it was a lot to ask. Not only was the guarantor required to put money on the

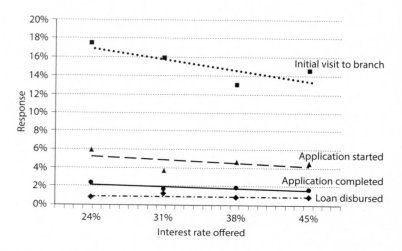

FIGURE 2. Progress towards a loan, by interest rate. From authors' own research.

line; it was also a hassle to do the paperwork, which required coming to the branch in person and providing extensive documentation to verify income or wealth sufficient to cover the borrower's payments.

A second challenge with the loan application was timing. Averaging about a month and a half from initial inquiry to loan disbursement, it simply took too long. Many applicants had time-sensitive needs; as their deadlines came and went and they remained "under review," many either withdrew their applications or just dropped off the map.

Together, these amounted to a narrow take-up funnel. For every 100 business owners that received an offer, about 15 responded by visiting an OISL branch. Of these, about 5 (4.7 percent) started an application, and only about 2 (1.8 percent) completed it. And of those 2, just 1 (0.9 percent) made it to the finish line and actually took a loan.

The upshot, evident to the naked eye in figure 2, was that the final number of clients receiving loans was too small to do any meaningful analysis about clients' sensitivities to different interest rates. And, critically, the total lending (about 30 loans) was immaterial to OISL from a bottom-line perspective, far too small to justify the large expenditure on door-to-door marketing.

WHAT WAS THE FAILURE?

On the surface, this is a simple case of *low participation*. Far fewer clients took loans than was projected in the pilot, slashing the study's power. There are two big reasons why this happened.

The first relates to the *research setting*. OISL's personal loan product, which had been developed just before the project began, *was not mature enough* to support the study. Everyone (wrongly) assumed that OISL's extensive experience processing and reviewing applications for group loans would translate to the individual lending context and that the application process would be smooth and efficient. Instead it turned out that loan requirements (i.e., guarantors and business inspections) unique to the new product, rather than interest rates, were driving determinants of take-up. Bottom line: regardless of the interest rate, although many expressed some desire for a loan, few were able to finish the application process.

That so many clients dropped out because of the sheer duration of the application process suggests a second kind of failure: the study placed *too high a burden on OISL's staff*. For the loan officers assigned to the project, individual lending was an added responsibility on top of their existing group lending portfolios. They had to make time for all the work of the study—meeting guarantors, visiting applicants' businesses—between holding group meetings, chasing down delinquent borrowers, and the like. Surely this contributed to the six-week average application time and the nearly 80 percent attrition rate between initiating an application and receiving a loan.

Note that none of these failures implies the product was forever a bust for OISL. In fact, the study revealed that some specific requirements were deal breakers for many potential clients, constraining qualified demand for their product. The fact that fourteen of fifteen applicants—who already had accepted the offered interest rate—fell through the cracks suggests there was room for improvement in converting would-be borrowers into actual clients. Further, it suggested that fine-tuning the interest rate was likely *not* a sufficient lever to do so—although it could be true that, once the necessary processes are in place to actually deliver loans, interest rates do matter.

LESSONS LEARNED + REMEDIATION

From a research perspective, one lesson is to assume less and observe more. In this case the faulty assumption was that few clients would be lost through the application process. The researchers would have done well to extend the pilot beyond marketing and potential clients' initial responses of visiting the branch. Had they followed the pilot clients all the way to loan disbursement, they might have uncovered some of the snags that drove so much attrition in the full study. It is natural to find the similarities between new and old routines and to see skills as transferable—OISL's loan officers were old hands at reviewing group loan applications; how different could this be?—but even subtle differences often prove substantive in the field.

A second general takeaway is to be wary of piling responsibilities onto existing partner staff. Adding new routines—in this case, marketing personal loans, reviewing new applications, and managing the resulting new borrowers—without intentionally creating space for it, perhaps by pulling back on other duties or offering incentives, presumes there is some freely available capacity prior to the study. Is that indeed the case? Even when staff members are clearly busy, it is tempting to believe they will go above and beyond on behalf of a worthy endeavor (and one's own research project always seems worthy). And the alternative of stretching an already tight budget to hire new staff often seems untenable. But plans that rely on full-time employees finding extra hours in their days often fall flat.

Although the jury remained out on the primary research question, the study did produce some conclusions. For one, there was a clear verdict on the application process: it was too stringent. Happily OISL took this to heart and relaxed the guarantor requirement in future versions of their individual loan product. The researchers pursued other settings to do this research as well. In an earlier study in South Africa, Karlan and Zinman found that lowering the interest rate for a consumer lender did increase quantity demanded—but not by enough to increase total revenue. But increasing the price drove people away and kept them away. The lender's best choice (to maximize profits) seemed to be to stay put. In Mexico, however, the results were starkly different and much longer run. After three years of a nationwide experiment, the lower interest rates led to *higher* revenue for the lender, meaning it was optimal for profits (and presumably for clients too!) to lower interest rates.[1]

CHAPTER 8

YOUTH SAVINGS

Real Money Drumming up Fake People

BACKGROUND + MOTIVATION

Simplistic wisdom, if there is such a thing, says the poor cannot save. The argument goes as follows: Being poor means having just enough to scrape by. Saving requires having something *more*, income beyond what is needed today for food, health care, school fees, and so forth. People may know they should put something aside for long-term needs or for protection if disaster hits, but when they receive money, immediate needs take precedence. As a result they are unprepared to meet these eventualities and shocks, and are left even more vulnerable than before. The cycle of underinvestment continues—a single-household "poverty trap."

Fortunately this myth has been effectively debunked[1] along with the simplistic logic behind it. The question is not whether the poor can save (they can) but how they can access tools to easily and safely put money away when they have it and withdraw it when they need it. For young people, it is not just about tools but also about building habits. Adopting saving behavior early could have important long-term impacts as they become spouses, parents, and providers.

Fundamentally there are two sets of policy levers that can be pushed to increase savings: supply side, that is, improving the accounts people can access, and demand side, that is, encouraging people to save more. Which approach would mobilize more savings? Could they be redundant? Are both approaches necessary to make any improvement? It is easy to imagine a story in which either one is ineffective on its own but together they change behavior. On the other hand, they could be substitutes, such that either one can change behavior but the two together are no better than each one individually. In 2009, researchers Julian Jamison from the Boston Federal Reserve Bank (now at the World Bank's "nudge" unit), Dean Karlan, and Jonathan Zinman of Dartmouth College designed an RCT to figure out which was the case.

STUDY DESIGN

The researchers worked with local partner organizations on two interventions: a simple group-based savings account and a youth-focused financial literacy curriculum made up of ten 90-minute sessions, to be held weekly for ten weeks. To recruit participants they partnered with the Church of Uganda, whose network of youth clubs counted thousands of members across the country. They chose 240 clubs, with about 20 members each, to take part in the study. These clubs were randomly assigned across four groups in a 2 x 2 design, which allowed the researchers to study the interventions both side by side and in combination.

They were interested in a range of outcomes, from knowledge about banks and finance, to attitudes about wealth, to actual behavior and performance as savers, borrowers, lenders, and earners. They planned to collect data on these indicators directly from members of the youth clubs with baseline and endline surveys, which were to be administered before and after the interventions, respectively. Respondents would have a chance to earn a nominal amount by completing the survey itself: in one of the modules a series of game-like tasks, designed to elicit preferences, were carried out with real money. On average, respondents earned just under $1 through this part of the survey.

IMPLEMENTATION PLAN

In terms of the failure we will discuss here, the details of financial literacy training and savings accounts do not matter. What does matter is the nature of the data the researchers planned to use.

As we saw briefly in chapter 4, administrative records—that is, data generated through participants' interactions with third parties—are preferred when available. In this case, researchers could analyze the impact of financial literacy on participants in the savings account treatment arm by tracking their account balances, but they had no such data for the other participants. And much of the other information they wanted was not already being captured anywhere. Nobody else was asking these teenage club members about their financial knowledge and attitudes. So they created a survey to supplement the administrative data.

Surveying can be fraught (see chapters 2 and 4), and despite real improvements, the process is still messy and imperfect. Surveys need to ask questions, but the very asking can influence respondents one way or another. The researchers in this case suspected respondents in the treatment group might feel pressured to give certain answers. Suppose the financial literacy training suggests participants should aspire to save more. When a survey, linked to the training, then asks them about their savings goals, naturally they might say what they think researchers want to hear, especially on highly subjective questions like those about attitudes. Meanwhile, those in the control group might have different expectations (or none at all) about what researchers want to hear. This can lead to a bias, called an *experimenter demand effect*.

There are two ways of dealing with this. First, and as above, use administrative data whenever possible. Second, separate data collection as much as possible from the delivery of the intervention. This minimizes the participants' perceptions that the two are linked. In credit impact studies in South Africa and the Philippines, researchers went so far as to hire the survey team entirely independently of the intervention, never revealing to the surveyors who the lending partner was. Thus, when they were conducting surveys, the surveyors had nothing to hide.

This study took both approaches but relied mostly on the second. The researchers created two separate field teams. First, a "survey" team conducted the baseline in May and June 2010. Next, a "treatment" team delivered the interventions from July to the following May. Finally, the "survey" team returned to do the endline from June through August 2011.

Since they did not overlap in the field, the two teams needed a way to verify that the right people received the right treatments between baseline and endline. They settled on the simple approach of having treatment team members take verbal attendance at club meetings where financial education sessions were delivered or where the savings account was offered. They could also use data collected in the baseline as security questions (for example, the participant's birthday, current school, or parents' jobs) to further confirm identities.

This approach has a clear trade-off. On one hand, separating the two is desirable: it helps mitigate the experimenter demand effect, that is, the risk that participants, knowing they are part of an experiment, change their survey responses in hopes of pleasing researchers or positioning themselves to be part of future studies. On the other hand, such separation is challenging for two reasons. First, it means more complexity, managing two field teams instead of one, and coordinating their activities. Second, it carries its own risk: if the connection is discovered, it may breed mistrust among participants.

From each of the 240 youth clubs, 12 members were randomly selected to complete the baseline and endline surveys. (Given the overall sample size and the fact that treatment was administered at the group level, for the analysis it was unnecessary to survey every member of every group.) The club leaders, who were aware of the whole setup, were asked to ensure the chosen 12 would be available for surveying and to otherwise be discreet.

WHAT WENT WRONG IN THE FIELD + CONSEQUENCES

Keeping track of individuals proved far more difficult than calling names, as club members attempted to cover up each other's absences. The project associate overseeing the fieldwork recalled instances when roll call unfolded roughly as follows:

"Marie!" Silence.

"Marie?" Silence.

"Marie Obua?" Rustling. A whisper. A girl toward the back of the room elbows her neighbor in the ribs. The neighbor's hand goes up. "Present."

"Marie Obua? Are you sure?"

Pause. ". . . Yes."

The facilitator leafs through the pages on his clipboard. "Marie, where are you attending school now?"

Coughing; clearing of throats. Murmuring fills the pause. "Marie" leans over to better hear her neighbor, who is whispering toward her. She straightens up. "I am at Saint Joseph's Secondary School."

. . . and so on.

Watching people struggle to remember "their own" personal details made it obvious something was amiss. But they were not in a position to call the club members liars outright. First, they might have been wrong in some cases: discrepancies on security questions could have been due to mistakes by the baseline survey team. Second, maybe the participants were just shy, a bit nervous about being called upon in a meeting like this. Third, doing so would have forced the surveyors to publicly acknowledge the connection between survey and treatment. So the team noted the strange phenomenon, alerted the researchers, and carried on.

The researchers set up meetings with a number of club leaders, who ultimately confirmed their suspicions. Club members had been talking—particularly those who had received (purportedly unrelated) visits from surveyors. Some had likely told their fellow members about the experience, and perhaps also about the money they had received through the survey. With that in mind, an absence by one of the twelve became a potential opportunity for another member to get in on the action by taking the other member's place. Hence the impersonations. In a couple cases it actually turned out that the club leaders—who were purportedly committed partners in the study—had put them up to it! Ironically, it appeared these leaders had themselves played into the experimenter demand effect: they were afraid that poor attendance by their members would reflect badly on the club and disappoint the researchers. Perhaps they imagined it would hurt their chances of being involved in valuable programs in the future.

Whether due to members or club leaders, the effect of spotty attendance was to dilute treatment. Where the intention was to study the impact of the complete ten-part financial education course, most members got considerably less: the estimated mean number of sessions attended was below five. And the rub is that, because of impersonations, official attendance records cannot say definitively who got what. This meant imperfect compliance could not be controlled for in analysis.

Though that round of surveying had been compromised, later the researchers returned for another wave of data collection, with no incentives for impersonations, an individualized approach to surveying (to avoid the roll call situation narrated earlier), and careful tracking of personal details to make sure identities were verified. Happily, their second effort was more successful.

WHAT WAS THE FAILURE?

The outermost phenomenon here is simple: subjects gamed the system of identity checks. If nothing else, it qualifies as a failure of *survey and measurement execution*. Experiments do not work when we collect data—especially attendance data that verify whether subjects have received treatment—from the wrong people.

A deeper question is whether there was a failure of *technical design* in this case, too. In light of the competing issues at play, it is hard to fault the researchers' plan. (Of course we may be biased, as one of the researchers is a coauthor of this book.) Given a setting where official documents are scarce—not all club members had government-issued picture ID cards, for instance—identifying and tracking individuals over time is always a challenge. Could the researchers have found better ways to follow respondents from the baseline, through treatment, and to the endline? Could they have done so without revealing the connection between survey and treatment?

The other candidate for a failure of *technical design* is the set of underlying incentives that led club members to behave badly in the first place. Leaving aside the few instances where the club leader encouraged members to impersonate, the simplest explanation here is money. The possibility of earning a couple dollars through the survey's preference-elicitation tasks proved compelling enough to shape subjects' behavior—a sobering reminder that nominal payments can have outsize influence in poor contexts.

LESSONS LEARNED + REMEDIATION

The first lesson is: build in (more!) safeguards against mistaken identity—and outright fraud. Using baseline survey data to create security questions is a good start, but it wasn't enough in this case. One could imagine using photographs, one-time authorization codes sent by SMS, or even fingerprints. IPA is constantly learning from failures such as these and improving its methods for collecting data in the field. These improvements are the lifeblood of field research.

More robust systems naturally carry their own challenges: they add layers of technological complexity, usually cost more, and can make participants uncomfortable. Club members might have balked at being asked to provide other identifying features such as a fingerprint scan to access a free and voluntary financial education course. The right level of security depends on the project, but it helps to consider a range and to have contingency plans should the initial protocol prove too weak or too strong.

One example of a successful pivot on this front comes from a project that offered counseling and cash grants to unemployed, homeless young men in Liberia from 2009 to 2012, evaluated by Chris Blattman of Yale University (now at Columbia University), Julian Jamison, Margaret Sheridan of Harvard Medical School and Boston Children's Hospital, and Tricia Gonwa of IPA (now at the World Bank). At $200, the cash grants were big enough to make researchers concerned about impersonation. Pre-piloting validated this concern: despite asking numerous security questions, it was clear some people were trying to game the system. In response, they adopted a stronger protocol for the full study, creating custom-made photo IDs for all participants. If this was a burden on participants, it was clearly outweighed by the value of the potential treatments: 99 of 100 subjects agreed to share their photo with the research team, and the impersonation problem was solved.

Back to the Ugandan case: Once it was clear that the participants understood the connection between treatment and survey, might the research team have done better to publicly acknowledge it and address the impersonation issue explicitly? There is no single right answer here, just trade-offs: Stay the course, or adapt? Hold up a simple (if shaky) front, or take the risk of revealing and explaining the connection between research and implementation?

A brief aside here for a reality check. How likely is it that subjects do not discover the connection between survey and treatment in a randomized trial like this one? At a minimum, survey participants will know they are part of a study because ethical research practice requires that all subjects give informed consent to share their data. Even if the data collection and intervention happen separately, as they did in this case, usually the experimental treatment is a departure from the status quo—a new offering or additional activity, a change in policy.

The youth clubs participating in this study had never before received financial literacy training or been marketed financial products. It is bound to raise eyebrows when such changes "just happen to" coincide with an unprecedented survey about financial attitudes and behaviors. And it is even more obvious if people notice the same research staff checking in on both survey and treatment teams, as is often the case given limited monitoring capacity in the field. In particular, it is hard for foreign researchers in developing countries to be discreet, as they often stick out like a sore thumb. Naturally it *can* happen, but to make it happen one likely needs to go to great lengths.

The last lesson here is about the underlying incentives that helped create the impersonation problem: the fact that only the twelve members being surveyed (and not the others in the group) had a chance of getting paid. What if this had not been the case? Why not simply use play money to ask the preference-elicitation questions? There is a growing literature[2] comparing hypothetical- and real-choice methods for learning individuals' preferences. The upshot is that methods using real money or goods are generally more predictive of individuals' actual behavior than hypothetical questions (like "How much would you pay for X?"). One literature review[3] found that subjects inflated values by about three times in hypothetical- versus real-choice settings.

One alternative would be to avoid questions about money, whether real or hypothetical. We could ask, for instance: " 'In general I am afraid of taking on risks.' Do you Strongly Agree, Agree, Neither Agree nor Disagree, Disagree or Strongly Disagree with that statement?" Individuals may actually grasp questions like these better than ones that ask about specific quantities (e.g., "Would you rather have $10 today or $12.50 in a week?"), but naturally it is difficult to use them to calibrate an economics model, as they do not yield specific numeric parameters. We also have yet to see sufficient research to understand which types of such qualitative questions best predict real behavior. More work is needed on this.

Another option in this case would have been to have *everyone* participate in the baseline survey (or at least the preference-elicitation exercise). Of course such additional surveying would have been costly and time-consuming. But it might have averted the impersonation problem.

Treating subjects differently who have great visibility into each other's lives—friends, classmates, neighbors, members of the same trade association or church—carries inherent risk. People talk. And usually they talk more to each other than to outside researchers. At some level this is unavoidable in an RCT, as some people will be assigned to treatment and others to control. But, where possible, these differences should not occur within a close-knit group. Researchers were wise to randomize treatment club by club rather than at the individual level. They might have gone one step further to design a survey process that was more uniform across all the members of each club.

CHAPTER 9

POULTRY LOANS

Trying to Fly without a Pilot

BACKGROUND + MOTIVATION

Many market vendors in developing countries seem stuck in a debt trap. A prototypical scenario involves a hardworking woman who comes to the market every day to sell vegetables. Arriving at the crack of dawn, she borrows $20 from a moneylender to buy stock for the day. Selling all her produce, she earns $30. Closing down in the evening, the moneylender visits her at her stall to collect $22. The next day—and the next, and the next—the drama plays out again.

A simple spreadsheet model paints a stark picture. Currently our vegetable seller pays $2 per day—20 percent of her profit—in interest. If she could save just a few cents a day and borrow less tomorrow, over (surprisingly little!) time she would be debt free, and every day she could put that additional $2 into her pocket instead—or into her highly productive business, where it could be turned into even more.

Why is it so hard to stay the course of saving and get out (or stay out) of debt? An insight from behavioral science offers a potential fix: maybe timing is the key. In the usual scenario, savings gets last dibs. As soon as earnings materialize, money-lenders swoop in to collect their payments. Next come living expenses. Last comes savings—if anything is left over. What if, instead, an opportunity to save came first?

Bindu Ananth from India's Institute for Finance and Management Research (IFMR), Sendhil Mullainathan from Harvard University, and Piyush Tantia from the behavioral design lab ideas42 wanted to find out. Searching for an industry where earnings naturally came in a lump sum that could be partially diverted to savings, they landed on sugarcane production. Then they conceived a credit-to-savings intervention: taking on farmers as clients, they could make loans of inputs for growing, arrange a buyer for the finished product, and set up a single payment from the proceeds to cover inputs for the next growing cycle, a loan payment, and a savings deposit. Over a few rounds of growing and selling, farmers would both establish a sustainable business and save their way out of debt.

Everyone was happy with the plan and they set about finding partner organizations to help with a pilot. They identified agricultural suppliers and buyers and engaged Sahastradhara KGFS, a local financial services organization that could make the loans. As they neared launch, though, one of the buyers balked. The researchers found themselves in a jam: having already identified a question, recruited partners, invested time and resources in planning, and secured funding for a study, they were not keen on letting the idea go.

Fortunately (or so it seemed) a solution appeared from a researcher at IFMR who had recently learned about a poultry supply company that sold chicks for raising into broilers. These particular chicks, a proprietary breed called Kuroilers, were supposed to be especially low-maintenance—able to scavenge for food and grow to full size even with imperfect care—an appeal-

ing feature, as many clients had limited or no experience raising poultry. The Kuroilers also grew faster than most breeds,
taking just four weeks to go from chicks to salable birds.

It looked like a clean swap: as with sugarcane there was a
regular and repeatable growth cycle—this one beginning with
chicks and coops, adding feed and water, and ending with a
sale of grown chickens. So they found a poultry distributor who
agreed to buy full-grown chickens at a fixed price, rejiggered
the plan to accommodate fowl instead of produce, and set out
to execute.

STUDY DESIGN

The final intervention was dubbed the Poultry Loan. It worked
as follows: On day one, clients received a disbursement from
Sahastradhara KGFS to buy coops and twelve Kuroiler chicks.
Two weeks later they received a second disbursement to buy
feed and a second set of chicks. By the end of the fourth week
ramp-up was complete: the chicks purchased on day one would
be full-grown. Every two weeks after that, clients would turn
over a new cycle, selling their grown chicks (for about $2 each)
to the distributor. With the proceeds in hand, they would make
a payment to Sahastradhara KGFS; buy new chicks (for about
$1 each) and additional feed; and still go home with some cash
in hand. Over the course of eight such cycles clients would pay
off their loans entirely, thus owning their poultry concerns free
and clear.

Though the Poultry Loan sounded like plain credit, it had
a savings component built in. Clients were quoted an interest
rate of 20 percent, but behind the scenes Sahastradhara KGFS
only charged 15 percent. The additional 5 percent would be diverted to a personal savings account. The accumulated savings
(of about $30) would be released upon completion of the tenth

cycle, giving clients a pot of money from which they could buy more chicks if they wished—no borrowing required.

With so many moving parts—suppliers, distributors, lender, farmers, chickens—the researchers wanted to see whether the Poultry Loan worked. Through an informational and promotional campaign, they recruited fifty participants willing to try poultry farming and launched a pilot. At this stage the research did not include an impact evaluation but just sought to determine whether the model was operationally viable. If the pilot proved successful, they planned to scale it up across Sahastradhara KGFS's nationwide network of branches. Only then would they consider a study sufficiently large to test the impacts of the Poultry Loan on clients' saving, borrowing, incomes, and the like.

IMPLEMENTATION PLAN

The linchpin of execution was the biweekly cycle turnover day, when most of the action occurred. Given the sheer number of transactions that had to be made—multiple clients collecting disbursements of coops, feed, and chicks; presenting chickens for sale; making loan payments—it could easily have ballooned into a daylong event. (Nobody was keen on that option.) Drawn from rural villages in the hills outside Uttarakhand, India, some clients lived hours from the nearest bank branch and did not want to lose a whole workday traveling to and from a distant meeting site. Nor would they want to subject their tender, just-bought chicks to the rigors of transport, which involved being confined with limited access to food and water.

To minimize inconvenience all around, a plan was developed that centered on roving trucks. On cycle turnover day, trucks would set out for the villages, laden with new chicks and feed and each carrying a representative of the distributor who was also empowered to collect loan payments on behalf of

Sahastradhara KGFS. At a predetermined collection point near each village, local clients could meet the trucks and do their business. This way, clients would spend less time traveling; poultry buyers would save Sahastradhara KGFS staff the trouble of making collections; and chicks would not have to endure long trips tucked into cloth sacks or the folds of clients' saris.

They planned to launch the pilot in February 2010, at the beginning of the dry season in the region, in the hopes that roads would remain passable and the remote villages would be accessible by truck through all ten cycles.

WHAT WENT WRONG IN THE FIELD + CONSEQUENCES

A complicated transition to new banking software delayed the launch until July 2010, just as the monsoon season began. When the pilot went live, the links in the poultry supply chain failed one by one. In a remarkably short time—just under two months—the project was abandoned.

The first link to fail was the chickens themselves. Too many died: pilot farmers found that three out of four survived, short of the 90 percent survival rate touted by the Kuroiler sellers. Come cycle turnover day, farmers had fewer birds to sell. And of the ones that survived all the way to fifty-day maturity, most weighed less than the advertised kilogram.

Maybe the Kuroiler folks had overpromised about the chickens, but an operational glitch compounded the problem. Trucks never made their rounds to clients' villages as planned; instead they just parked outside the nearest Sahastradhara KGFS branch and waited for clients to come to them. (Interviews after the fact never found exactly how or why this key component of the implementation plan ran awry. The researchers had assurances from their local counterparts that the trucks would rove.) Because of the distances clients had to travel, chicks endured hours of waiting and jostling transport without food or water. In all likelihood, these traumatic days contributed to chicks' lower survival rates and weights.

Fewer and, more important, undersized chickens strained relations with the distributor, who understandably did not want to pay the pre-agreed fixed price for birds that were smaller than advertised. All of this added up to a bumpy ride for clients: arriving with armfuls of fowl on cycle turnover day, some were offered less than they expected per chicken, and others were turned away entirely. The consequent revenue shortfall meant some were then unable to buy feed for the coming cycle or make complete loan payments.

All these unfortunate dominoes fell remarkably quickly. By the fourth cycle—which, given the two-cycle ramp-up period, was just the second time clients had grown birds to sell—the distributor balked altogether and canceled its commitment to buy chickens, citing low weight. With this critical link in the supply chain broken, Sahastradhara KGFS quickly put the pilot on hold, where it has remained ever since.

WHAT WAS THE FAILURE?

First we should be clear about one thing: this case *isn't* a failure, strictly speaking. It is actually a prime example of an appropriate pilot! Sahastradhara KGFS was wise to test Poultry Loans with just fifty participants instead of launching it as a retail product right out of the gate. Doing so gave them a chance to work out the kinks on a small sample. That said, even the limited pilot offers failures worth discussing, all related to the *research setting*.

First, at the front line of implementation, Sahastradhara KGFS's unexpectedly lengthy software update caused a *timing* problem. Delaying launch from February until the beginning of July meant they missed the dry season and got the monsoon instead. Everything is more difficult amid daily downpours: constructing coops, keeping feed from washing away, driving lumbering trucks over rutted dirt (or mud) roads to rural villages, meeting outdoors.

Second, the complexity of the intervention made it challenging to roll out all at once. The individual components of the Poultry Loan—a microloan, a "chicken-farm-in-a-box" type enterprise product, a supply chain with distributors and buyers—were interdependent, so that failure of any one piece would (and did) bring all the rest down with it. None of the components was totally novel, but Sahastradhara KGFS was new to the world of chicken farms and supply chains. Given their inexperience, the Poultry Loan was an *immature product* to study. (Though, again, we salute them and the researchers for piloting instead of rushing to a full-scale experiment.)

The third lesson goes back to the beginning of the story, before Poultry Loans were even an idea. The researchers had observed a problem (debt traps), imagined a possible solution (credit with a built-in enterprise component and a savings component that helped borrowers climb out of debt), identified a setting where their solution could work (sugarcane farming), and secured grant funding for a study. When the sugarcane plan fell through, they found themselves in a tight spot: funds committed, time and resources invested in planning, funder reporting deadline looming, and nothing to show for it. They *failed to acknowledge these sunk costs* and instead tried to dig their way out by hastily pulling together the Poultry Loan product.

LESSONS LEARNED + REMEDIATION

As in many cases we discuss, the first lesson here is to do more, and more granular, pre-testing. A complex intervention like the Poultry Loan might have been best served by a range of separate, focused pre-pilots. For instance, before launching with fifty clients, the researchers could have asked a smaller group to simply raise Kuroiler chicks—no credit or financing involved. This might have revealed the lower-than-advertised survival rate and the difficulty in getting chickens to reach the one-kilogram mark. They might also have observed the poultry buyer for a few weeks to observe his willingness to purchase birds of different sizes.

A deeper lesson here, from behavioral psychology and prospect theory, is to be on the lookout for loss frames and, when they arise, to proceed with caution. This case offers two relevant examples: timing and the last-minute substitution of poultry for sugarcane.

It was a deliberate (and wise!) choice to schedule the study around the monsoon season. When an incidental software issue foiled that plan, it triggered a loss frame among the research team: We are going to miss our window of opportunity; what should we do? The right decision may have been to wait—even if meant postponing for months, shuffling field staff from one project to another, or the like. Of course the real costs of such delays and operational headaches should have been weighed against the likelihood that the weather would actually derail the study. The point is not that they made the wrong choice but rather that their judgment was likely influenced by the context in which they found themselves. People in a loss frame tend to choose riskier behaviors—in this case to forge ahead in spite of the weather.

A similar explanation fits the hasty conception of the Poultry Loans product in the first place. Fixed on an idea, with a grant disbursed and partially spent, and a project team ready to go in the field, the dissolution of the original sugarcane plan triggered a similar loss frame: We are going to lose our opportunity to learn, balk on this grant, and disappoint our funder; what can we do? From this position, almost any alternative must have looked attractive that promised to salvage the bones of the original plan—hence the swapping out of sugarcane for poultry.

Another option—no doubt also fraught—would have been a conversation with the funder and a request for an extension, help finding a new project site, or other adjustment to the grant. Again, we do not mean to suggest that the researchers made the wrong choice but rather to note the challenges that anyone in their position would face in making a decision.

CHAPTER 10

CHILD HEALTH AND BUSINESS TRAINING WITH CREDIT

No Such Thing as a Simple Study

BACKGROUND + MOTIVATION

Delivering training or education in conjunction with micro-credit is an appealing proposition for a variety of reasons. First, there may be business benefits for the lender: financial literacy or entrepreneurial training could help borrowers become more successful in business, increasing the likelihood that they will be able to repay their loans. Other types of training could impact the bottom line indirectly. Health or hygiene education, for instance, could lead to a lower incidence of illness for clients and their families, meaning fewer days of missed work and, again, better chances of making payments on time.

Second, education may simply make people's lives better, in terms of financial security or health—a worthy end in itself, and potentially compelling to mission-driven microfinance institutions or aligned funders. Finally, from a societal perspective, packaging education with microcredit may be an efficient alternative to providing such services separately, as it leverages both the infrastructure and incentives microfinance institutions have already built. It is often difficult to convene people regularly and for hours at a time. Yet group-based micro-credit organizations are often doing that anyway, gathering clients for regular repayment meetings. Thus microcredit can be a channel for reaching people for other purposes. (Naturally there is a trade-off here. Piggybacking additional services on microcredit implies giving those services to borrowers instead of to a more expansive group.)

One microfinance institution (MFI for short) provided an opportunity to learn more about these trade-offs. Around 2000, they began developing educational supplements for their client base of poor women on the topics of infant/child health and business training. They adapted materials from an international nonprofit headquartered in the United States, which had developed training curricula for use in dozens of developing countries. They thoughtfully tweaked their materials to fit their audience—for instance, changing characters' names and replacing mentions of smoothies, little known to their clients, with examples of a dessert drink that was extremely popular locally.

With tailored materials ready, the MFI launched the program in about half of its branches, using an "integrated model" in which loan officers delivered the trainings during their weekly repayment meetings. Clients at one branch were surveyed about the new program, and those who had received training had only positive comments about their experience. By 2003 the MFI was considering expanding credit-with-education across all its remaining branches. There were still important open questions: How much would education impact clients' business and health outcomes? Would offering education attract new clients, or induce existing clients to stay around longer, or some combination of the two? Would clients share what they learned with family and friends, thus (indirectly) extending the program's reach? The possible expansion offered a prime opportunity for a rigorous test of these questions, and the MFI partnered with Xavier Giné of the World Bank and Dean Karlan to conduct an evaluation.

STUDY DESIGN

The MFI and the researchers conceived an RCT to compare the business and health trainings side by side. They targeted 12 bank branches, which covered 680 borrowing groups of about 30 clients each, and randomly assigned groups to receive business training, health training, or neither (the control group).

One advantage of RCTs is that as long as the sample size is large enough, as it was in this case, random assignment will produce on average similar treatment and control groups. (Ideally one has *some* demographic data at the start, even if not a full household survey, to verify that randomization has indeed balanced the groups along basic observable characteristics.) Thus extensive baseline surveying is not essential; but the range of data collected at baseline may limit the kinds of tests researchers can run. For instance, one can still ask whether the program works better for older versus younger, or those with more education versus less, or those with roofs versus those without (a proxy for poverty, but make sure to check when the roof was built). But one likely cannot ask whether the program works better for those who are happier or for those who have more power in the household, since those are difficult questions to ask in recall.

Thus the study proceeded, without a full baseline survey. The researchers did not have financing committed for the study beforehand, beyond some funding for monitoring the experimental protocols and coordinating with the MFI's management team on execution. They planned to use monitoring results from the experiment to demonstrate to funders that they could buy a study "on the cheap," since the experiment had already occurred, and all that was needed was a follow-up survey. Although project planning is easiest when everything is known up-front, this is not uncommon: to have enough money to start a project, knowing that funds can likely be raised for low-risk, high-return opportunities.

The financial literacy and health curricula were roughly the same length, and both were fairly extensive: business training had 40 modules and health had 42. Business topics included planning, money management, and how to increase sales; health training was squarely aimed at mothers, focusing on infant and child health and family planning. Loan officers would conduct the trainings during their groups' weekly repayment meetings.

To understand the benefits to clients, they planned to track a variety of outcomes. They would use administrative data for personal finances: loan repayment rates, loan sizes requested, savings balances, and loan-to-loan retention. To see whether clients had adopted key lessons from the trainings, they designed an endline survey that asked about business status— including revenues, use of processes like record keeping, and survival—and health outcomes like children's weight and incidence of diarrhea.

IMPLEMENTATION PLAN

In order to minimize confusion and limit the burden on the MFI's staff, randomization was structured so that each loan officer had only one topic to deliver. A typical loan officer handled twelve borrowing groups, of which four would be assigned to control and the remaining eight to either business or health. To prepare, loan officers completed a four-day intensive training course covering both curriculum content and facilitation techniques—again, most loan officers were new to teaching.

Business and health intensives ran three times each, on a staggered schedule so that branch managers could cover for loan officers while they were attending. The intensives were offered over the course of two months, with loan officers attending as their schedules permitted.

As soon as a loan officer had completed her four-day course, she was free to begin the trainings with her assigned borrowing groups. With a lot of material to cover, there was a fair amount of flexibility in the training schedule: knowing that some meetings would end up being used for other activities like opening and closing out loans, tracking down delinquents, and the like, each group had 12–13 months (i.e., 50+ weekly meetings) to complete the 40 or 42 modules of their assigned curriculum. Loan officers could decide to skip some weeks at their discretion.

The research team's presence was concentrated toward the beginning and end of the study. They had led the up-front design, planned to visit the field in the summer for a midpoint audit, and would supervise the endline survey and data analysis. However, compared with most other studies discussed in this book, they had only a small role in the day-to-day operations during the period of treatment delivery. It is worth noting that this was a compromise: the researchers had offered up additional staff to assist with monitoring, but the MFI's management team declined, citing what they saw as a volatile security situation in the area where the study was set to run. They did not want the additional burden of securing the safety of visiting researchers and were confident they could manage the implementation largely on their own.

WHAT WENT WRONG IN THE FIELD + CONSEQUENCES

The study launched as planned in March, loan officers attended their four-day intensives, and they began delivering trainings to their groups. It turned out to be an even busier time than expected. In a decision unrelated to the study, the MFI changed a longstanding policy: in an effort to make their loans more accessible, they decreased the length of the orientation course for first-time borrowers from twenty-four hours to eight. That meant less hassle for new clients, but it also meant loan officers had less time to hammer home the importance of attendance at weekly meetings and making payments on time.

Following the policy change, repayment rates fell sharply. Whether the drop was *caused* by the change one cannot say for sure, since drops in repayment can occur organization-wide for myriad reasons; but the MFI's management team, using their judgment and experience, attributed the drop to the policy change and their underlying effort to expand their client base. Lower repayment rates meant loan officers had to spend more meeting time chasing delinquents and admonishing their groups—both of which had the potential to crowd out health and business training.

Nonetheless, all reports on the research and education component were positive: everything seemed to be proceeding as planned. Yet there were no monitoring data to confirm this and no full-time staff on the ground working side by side with the MFI to observe what was happening—only conversations with the management team. So the researchers set up a field audit by bringing on a summer intern, Nathanael Goldberg (who later joined IPA full-time and is now leading its work on social protection). Nathanael visited in midsummer, about four months into the study. Over the course of three busy weeks he crisscrossed the study area to observe the meetings of 34 borrowing groups that had been assigned to treatment.

He discovered that many groups were far behind on training. Some loan officers had clearly taken their discretion over scheduling to heart; they had begun skipping trainings right out of the gate. With around 50 meetings to complete 40 modules, they should have conducted trainings at about 80 percent of their meetings. Equivalently, on any given day about 80 percent of groups meeting should have been holding trainings. But of the 34 meetings he dropped in on, only 22 were. (And even that number was inflated, as Nathanael made some last-minute changes to his itinerary when he discovered some groups he had hoped to observe were not meeting at all.) Among the 22 that were holding sessions, the median group was on just its fourth module—about one-tenth through the curriculum, though they were over three-tenths of the way through the implementation period.

In terms of the experiment, this amounted to a dilution of treatment: only a portion of the groups assigned to receive training were actually receiving it, and often at lower intensity than was intended. This weakened the study's statistical power—the ability to detect effects of reasonable size, given the size of the study—but not enough to compromise it entirely. And, frankly, if such dilution is typical of the way training would *actually* be rolled out within a microcredit organization, it could generate a more accurate measure of the impact one could expect to see. It is the difference between asking "What is the impact of training?" and "What is the impact of training as it could plausibly be delivered by a microcredit organization, with all its competing responsibilities and duties?" Implicitly, the researchers were asking the second, perhaps more policy-relevant question. As such, less-than-perfect adherence to the training actually was likely appropriate, if it more closely reflected operational realities.

After the field audit, though, a more serious problem arose. Word came to the research team that some loan officers were conducting trainings with some of their borrowing groups that had been assigned to control—a phenomenon known as contamination. The flipside of the dilution Nathanael had observed, this similarly decreases the statistical power of a study. But compromising the control group is not "natural" in the way that reduced training in the treatment group might be. That both were happening was alarming, and the team set out to investigate. The staff member in charge of the credit-with-education program did a broad audit of borrowing groups in the study and sent the raw data to the researchers.

What they saw confirmed their fears. Treatment and control assignments were now being ignored almost completely. Only about half of the borrowing groups assigned to get health or business training were actually getting it; and about half of the remaining groups were getting one or the other training, though they should have gotten none. There was basically no difference between treatment and control. The study was over. With little hope of a result, everyone agreed to abandon the project. There was one minor consolation: not much was lost from a budgetary perspective, as no baseline survey had been conducted.

WHAT WAS THE FAILURE?

Why did treatment assignments get ignored? One immediate reason was that front-line staff members involved in the study faced *competing priorities*. As microlenders first and foremost, the MFI's management team was, for good reason, concerned with clients' repayment; and they encouraged loan officers to care about it, too. When push came to shove, they would prioritize their core job of making and collecting on loans over the new and additional job of delivering educational material. The MFI's decision to shorten new client orientation from twenty-four hours to eight likely added to this tension. As noted before, we cannot say for sure the two are causally related, but with repayment rates at their lowest levels in years, loan officers found themselves tasked with much of the legwork to stanch the repayment crisis just as they were expected to learn and launch a new line of services.

The underlying failure is that both problems—missed trainings and trainings given to the wrong groups—went unchecked for so long. If loan officers had been more aware of and invested in the research or managers more vigilant—or better yet had dedicated research staff been on-site to monitor and advocate throughout implementation—they might have caught these challenges and addressed them before it was too late.

LESSONS LEARNED + REMEDIATION

While the outward phenomenon in this case—contamination—was different from others we discuss in the book, researchers' anecdotes from the field suggest a familiar root cause: the study was one among many activities for the MFI at the time, and either loan officers did not understand the importance of following protocols faithfully or it did not take precedence over other priorities. Without a consistent champion on the front lines the study simply fell through the cracks.

In addition to the challenges caused by competing priorities, normal staff turnover between the launch of the study and the field audit meant that some of the loan officers tasked with delivering trainings had been replaced by the time Nathanael made his observations. When he arrived, he found that these new employees had not been briefed on the education initiative or trained to deliver the educational material.

These all point to the need for closer oversight on studies and for research staff on the ground to work with partners through the nitty-gritty implementation details. This can be hard to arrange. Budgets may be tight, or a partner may insist that their staff can do it themselves, as the MFI did in this case. Sometimes we as researchers fall into thinking we do not need it: "What we want to do here is not so complicated. We are just randomizing one piece of one product." We have learned (sometimes the hard way) that this perspective is usually wrong.

It is sometimes possible to truly automate the research so that it can happen without impinging on—or even better, so it streamlines—the operations of the partner organization. (Imagine, for instance, an intervention that sought to affect deposit and withdrawal behavior simply by changing the order or wording of options on ATM menu screens. No ongoing staff involvement required!) That is a great option when available; but it is the exception, not the rule. Even seemingly simple tasks usually involve active effort from many people, and for most of them our study is not the most important thing on their (typically full) plates. If we want follow-through given these constraints, we need to be hands-on, engaging with all levels of partner staff, keeping their attention on it, and explaining why and how the research is being done—how it can help them do their work better.

Two final notes on the funding discussion.

First, the researchers tried to bootstrap the setup of a project, knowing if the setup was successful they could raise funds for measuring the outcomes. Alas, bootstrapping the setup cost them dearly; they made a clear mistake by not staffing the project with the proper support in the field monitoring the project, working daily with the partner. Lesson learned.

Second, ironically, the lack of funding did make the mishap less painful, in that no donor money was wasted on a baseline survey. Although much can be learned from baseline surveys, this is still a relevant lesson: when there is uncertainty about the execution of a randomized trial, first demonstrate that the experiment itself is working, then raise funds for the endline. (For short-run experiments, given the often lengthy grant cycles at foundations, this advice may not apply.) If you do take this approach, support the project sufficiently on the ground to ensure a smooth implementation.

BUNDLING CREDIT AND INSURANCE

Turns Out More Is Less

BACKGROUND + MOTIVATION

Everybody faces unexpected shocks. A bout of sickness means missing a week's work and wages; a home or car damaged by a storm means needing to pay for repairs. These are inconveniences for all; but for the poor, who have the slimmest cushions of wealth and income to help absorb and rebound from such shocks, they can be much more. Facing pressing needs with little or no money to spare, people are forced into painful trade-offs: A roof over your head or food on your table? Surgery for your child or school fees?

In light of this reality, health insurance would seem to be a promising intervention, enabling the poor to distribute risk and smooth out shocks. But efforts to introduce insurance to the poor in developing countries have faced two obstacles. First, demand is generally low,[1] dampened by consumers' limited awareness and understanding of insurance products, liquidity constraints, and behavioral biases that favor current, salient needs over long-term health. Low demand may also simply reflect a lousy product: insurance policies will hold little value for consumers when the health services they cover are of low quality.[2] Second, concerns about adverse selection and moral hazard squeeze the supply side, keeping many insurers out of the market altogether and leading others to offer only rudimentary, "tamper-proof" products like indexed weather insurance policies.

One possible way around these two obstacles is to bundle policies with other products in hopes of attracting customers not currently seeking insurance (but who could still benefit from coverage), thus creating a viable pool of clients for insurers. In 2006, researchers Abhijit Banerjee and Esther Duflo of MIT and Richard Hornbeck of Harvard partnered with SKS Microfinance (then India's largest microfinance institution) and insurer ICICI-Lombard to test this theory by adding a mandatory health insurance policy to SKS microloans.

STUDY DESIGN

The researchers designed a randomized trial to take place in rural villages across India where SKS made microloans. In treatment villages, SKS would introduce mandatory bundling of a basic ICICI-Lombard health insurance policy for all borrowers. In control villages, SKS would not offer health insurance at all.

Once they introduced bundled insurance policies, the first thing to watch was enrollment: How many (and which) SKS customers would continue to take loans under the new regime? Second, researchers planned to compare customers' health and health care experiences, as well as loan repayment performance, across the treatment and control villages. They hoped to answer three questions: When insurance is bundled with a microloan, is there evidence of adverse selection in the resulting pool of clients? When people get insurance, how does it impact their investment choices? How does it impact what they do when they get sick?

IMPLEMENTATION PLAN

The partner organizations agreed to divide the work of providing insurance. ICICI-Lombard handled the back end, designing and underwriting the policies. The insurance itself was simple and limited, covering only hospitalizations and maternity expenses. A typical policy cost about $13—an actuarially fair price—and premium payments were rolled into customers' existing schedule of weekly loan installments.

SKS agreed to handle all the client-facing work of marketing and administration: educating borrowers about the policy, managing initial enrollment, processing claims, and collecting premium payments. Given SKS's average loan size at the time (just over $200) and its prevailing interest rate (about 24 percent APR), from a typical customer's perspective adding the $13 insurance policy was equivalent to raising the interest rate by a quarter—a significant jolt, it would soon become clear.

The researchers worked with the partners to identify 201 eligible rural villages where SKS was already operating. They randomly assigned 101 villages to treatment and the remainder to control. SKS planned to roll out bundled insurance to all clients in the treatment villages beginning in June 2007. That meant insurance would be both tacked onto all existing loans and built into any new loans made from that point forward.

In an effort to smooth the introduction of bundling, SKS also developed a pre-launch education campaign, which ran from December 2006 to March 2007. SKS staff spoke to clients about the insurance policy, provided supporting written materials, and screened a video that walked through some likely scenarios where the policy could be used and showed how to file claims.

WHAT WENT WRONG IN THE FIELD + CONSEQUENCES

SKS's bundling of insurance with microloans proved so problematic that, at the end of the day, there were not enough insured clients for researchers to study the impact of getting insurance on health experience or financial performance. This happened in a few stages.

First, borrowers hated the insurance mandate. Those with a loan underway, who (understandably) believed they had locked in their price and terms, were now being forced to pay extra for insurance policies they had never asked for—and they made a stink about it. In response to vehement client complaints, SKS quickly moved to relax its mandatory enrollment rule: instead of adding insurance onto *all existing and new* loans, they decided to limit the requirement to *new* loans only. At this point, SKS clients in treatment villages with loans outstanding as of June 2007 would be required to buy insurance only if (and when) they paid off the remainder of their current loans and decided to renew.

Many clients so disliked being forced to buy insurance that they chose not to renew their SKS loans. In control villages, about seven in ten renewed; in treatment villages, where the insurance mandate prevailed, the figure fell to about five in ten.

Chastened by client dropout in addition to continued complaints, SKS relaxed the insurance mandate even further: in October 2008, they announced that insurance would be completely voluntary. By this point the program was on the ropes. Not only were clients frustrated, but the partnership between

SKS and ICICI-Lombard was further strained by allegations that the insurance was not working as it was supposed to.

Indeed, it was not. The final problem with the rollout was the administration of the policies. For many clients who actually enrolled, the insurance coverage never materialized! There may have been names on the register and premiums paid, but so few claims were filed that it became clear something was seriously wrong. Follow-up interviews bore this out: purportedly insured clients explained they had never received insurance cards or other policy documentation and were never shown how to file claims. (It remains unclear how SKS's education campaign missed them.) For all intents and purposes, these people never got insurance, despite having purchased it.

These problems—sudden policy changes following client complaints, falling rate of loan renewal, and administrative errors—turned the experiment on its head. The initial vision was that bundling insurance would create a viable pool of insured microcredit clients to study; the actual effect was that bundling insurance drove clients away from microcredit. As a result, the researchers could not investigate adverse selection or moral hazard as they had initially intended.

Luckily they *did* produce some knowledge out of this experience, though it was not the knowledge they had initially sought. As it played out, the insurance mandate functioned as a (randomly applied) "shock" that led treatment-group clients to borrow less than their control-group counterparts. As such, the study could be seen as a sort of inverted impact-of-credit experiment: instead of the usual design, where the treatment group gets credit and control does not, in this case the treatment group actually got *less* credit and the control group more. The researchers could then estimate the impact of a contraction of credit on people near the margin of deciding whether to borrow or not.

WHAT WAS THE FAILURE?

The obvious failure here is *low participation* after randomization. With considerable time and effort already sunk into identifying 201 villages, assigning each to treatment or control, and conducting a baseline survey, so few clients ultimately ended up insured that the sample was insufficient to support a strong test of the research questions.

The deeper question is *why* low participation became an issue. This points to two contributing failures. First, there was a *partner organization burden around learning new skills*. As post-interviews with dissatisfied clients revealed, many SKS loan officers turned out to be lousy insurance salesmen. Some neglected to explain important procedures and details about the insurance policies to customers; others failed even to get enrolled clients their ID cards and other policyholder materials.

Clearly, one element of this case is a pure demand story: a surprisingly large subset of clients simply did not want to buy insurance. But why did this fact catch everybody by surprise? The answer, and the second contributing thread of failure here, can be traced all the way back to the project's inception. Before this study began, SKS had never bundled insurance with its loans. In terms of *research setting*, they were dealing with an *immature product*. Since neither the insurance policy itself nor the mandate that all borrowers buy insurance had been road-tested, they could not be certain how clients would react. Had they the chance to see the bundled product in the marketplace first—by running a limited pre-pilot, say—they might have had more realistic expectations for the way it would be received.

LESSONS LEARNED + REMEDIATION

One lesson to be drawn from this case is about the value of small-scale pre-testing before embarking on a full study. Pre-testing sometimes seems unnecessary, especially when the intervention being tested is not completely novel. (In this case SKS and other similar microloans were already widely used; and insurance was familiar, if not terribly popular, as a stand-alone product in rural Indian villages.) And in terms of the project life cycle, the best time to pre-test—after the intervention and experimental protocols are clearly defined, but before launch—often feels inopportune. By this juncture, researchers and partners alike have invested time and resources to develop an implementation plan and are excited to see it roll out. Adding a step that opens that plan up to revision, and could potentially take everyone back to the drawing board, might seem politically untenable.

Still, pilots are highly valuable. Unless you have access to data from an analogous setting—a similar study or product from a similar context—pre-testing or small-scale piloting is the best way to preview take-up rates and reveal operational hiccups that could arise during implementation.

Such pre-tests could prompt challenging conversations with partners. Suppose in this case there had been a pre-pilot, and it revealed clients' strong aversion to insurance. With a sample drawn from SKS's customer base, bottom-line consequences—angering and driving away clients, for example—are inherently in play. The (thorny) question for SKS would have been: "Is it worth potentially angering our clients and jeopardizing our business in order to help generate rigorous evidence and knowledge that could be valuable both to us and to the field?"

Pre-testing or none, there was no hiding from this question; angry clients brought it to SKS's doorstep when they bristled at the launch of insurance bundling. The path SKS took—softening the insurance mandate to new loans only, and finally making insurance optional altogether—might indeed have been a smart compromise under the circumstances. Unfortunately they made those decisions unilaterally, without consulting the research team, and likely without fully appreciating their potential to undermine the experiment. Unaware that such policy changes were coming, the researchers had no chance to alter the study's design accordingly. Instead they could only sort through the debris and try their best to extract some interesting insights—which they successfully did with the reverse-impact-of-credit approach they ultimately took.

We have talked a lot about how not to run a field study. But what about the positive question: How *do* you run one? In this conclusion and the appendix that follows we will offer some direct answers—though we stop far short of a complete how-to guide—and point you to additional resources that provide more detail.

First, to recap the "mantras" from part 1.

Mantra #1: Thou shalt have a well-understood context and an intervention that maps sensibly to a plausible theory of change. Think about where, when, and with whom you will run your experiment. Make sure these parameters fit the underlying idea or theory you intend to test. Understand the local environment: Is your experiment logistically feasible here and now? Pre-test whenever possible to confirm. Beware rushing to the field with a half-baked intervention.

Mantra #2: Thou shalt attend to technical but important details like survey design, timing, sample size requirements, and randomization protocols. Every question in a survey should have a purpose. Be mindful that subtle features of a survey like response scales and order of questions can influence the results. Instructions regarding who should be surveyed (and when and how) are just as important as what you ask. Double-check the nuts and bolts of experimental design, random assignment, and sampling strategies.

Mantra #3: Thou shalt have a willing and able implementing partner.

Participating in research is almost always a heavier lift than partners imagine at first. Be sure they understand what it will take. If the study will require some employees to assume additional or different duties, ensure they are given both the training and the bandwidth to take them on. Cultivate buy-in from senior management down to the front-line managers and employees who will participate in implementation. Know when to walk away from a failing partnership.

Mantra #4: Thou shalt collect data carefully.

Make an intentional decision about how, and how much, to incorporate technology into your survey. Manage the survey process closely, with eyes and ears on the ground. Train and observe surveyors well. Check data as they come in and audit continuously. Address problems with surveys or surveyors immediately, before they snowball.

Mantra #5: Thou shalt reduce the implementer's predicted participation rates by half, or maybe even more.

Do not assume people will sign up to receive a program or service, even if it *seems* like they should. Avoid taking partners' (or anybody's) word for it—find out directly whenever possible by piloting or otherwise gauging demand for your intervention. Ensure that enough people meet your eligibility criteria to achieve the sample size you need.

A note that cuts across the mantras: as the cases in part 2 showed, organizational challenges during implementation (as opposed to mistakes in experimental design or analysis) were often key contributors to research failures. In recent years, a line of operations research projects, often in settings and with partners much like the ones described in this book, have begun to focus on organizational traits like management processes and employee incentives. These studies aim to understand how tweaks to such features could improve the delivery of *any* programs and services. Research like this is much needed and should help avert future failures of all types—not just with evaluative research but also with simple and complex program implementation.

Beyond these few lessons are some more comprehensive resources. As randomized trials in economics have grown since the early 2000s, the field has begun to distill best practices and create basic tool kits to guide researchers and practitioners as they undertake studies. One of the first examples was the 2008 paper "Using Randomization in Development Economics Research: A Toolkit" by Esther Duflo and Rachel Glennerster (both of MIT) and Michael Kremer (Harvard). The recent *Running Randomized Evaluations: A Practical Guide* by Glennerster and Takavarasha (2013) is the most comprehensive "how-to" manual we are aware of with an emphasis on developing countries. Similarly comprehensive, *Field Experiments* by Alan Gerber and Donald Green (2012) is more focused on political science examples, but the lessons clearly generalize. Finally, the Research Resources section of J-PAL's website also includes up-to-date materials from both J-PAL and IPA on topics from theories of change to data management.

But there is not yet a standard practical curriculum for would-be field researchers, one that goes beyond the technical aspects on which academics often focus. Lab scientists, even at the undergraduate level, are explicitly trained in how to handle beakers and test tubes, how to calibrate measuring devices, and exactly how to record and report data. At present, field methods classes are not part of the curriculum in most economics programs—no required training teaches students how to handle survey data, how to pilot, and so forth. Though it is no substitute for such a class, the checklist that follows captures some of the basic lessons we have learned about running experiments in the field to tackle questions in social science.

The checklist starts with the pre-project steps: making sure the setting is right, the budget is appropriate, the staffing is right, human subjects protocols are set, and there is a clear theory of change that makes sense. Once working with a partner, for most projects a memorandum of understanding can go a long way toward helping everyone know what they have agreed to do and what rights they have. This is often nonbinding in that there are no monetary penalties for deviations, but it is a helpful way to make sure everyone agrees on what is going to be done. A small but important side note: this is also a critical juncture to make clear that the researchers have intellectual freedom to report the results, whatever they are. (Researchers often sign away the right to name the parties, which is fine, but ought never to sign away the right to report the lessons learned, as doing so sometimes will limit the world's ability to learn and, more selfishly, will adulterate the credibility of the researcher's other reports.) We then detail critical steps for designing and executing a survey and day-to-day issues to consider for managing projects.

For readers interested in diving deeper—which we strongly recommend if you are planning on either being a field researcher or collaborating with one—a list of further reading is available on IPA's website at http://www.poverty-action.org /karlanappel_failedresearchprojects.

The appendix intentionally omits topics economists and social scientists typically do learn in graduate school, such as: have a specific and testable theory, do power calculations carefully, think deliberately about alternative causal mechanisms, think hard about measurement, include subtreatments to tease apart mechanisms.

One final, and hopefully obvious, caveat: this checklist is not exhaustive. There are far more ways to fail than we address here, many already known and far more as yet undiscovered. To echo the introduction, all researchers will experience failure at some point. The best we can hope for is to help reduce the proportion of research failures that arise from predictable or avoidable causes. As Jim Canales, president of the Barr Foundation, has said: "It is not just to avoid reinventing the wheel. We want to make sure we don't reinvent the potholes."[1]

We encourage all the less-than-perfect readers out there to join us in reporting failures like the ones we share here. Working with colleagues David McKenzie and Berk Özler of the World Bank, we have started a series of posts on the World Bank development blog. Others can submit their stories. If enough do this, we plan to spin it out as a stand-alone blog, for people's failures to live forever in infamy (and maybe even compete with each other for "likes"). Please help us—and all researchers—by sharing your own juicy failures from which everyone can learn.

CHECKLIST FOR AVOIDING FAILURES

PRE-PROJECT PLANNING AND PREPARATION

❑ *Validating your assumptions*: Check your assumptions with focus groups and/or descriptive data. Do not rely on third-party data for this unless you are highly confident in it.

❑ *Budgeting*: Build a comprehensive budget, covering every stage of the project.

❑ *Recruiting and hiring research assistants*: Beyond technical skills, look for:

- Emotional maturity—the ability to cope with a challenging environment and remain motivated amid changes to schedules and plans;
- Experience in the country or region where you plan to work, or at least in some developing-country setting if possible;
- Management skills required to support surveyors and other field staff;

- Good communicators who can maintain rapport with partners and pass *the right* information to the research team regularly and quickly but not overdo it.

❑ *Human subjects*: Take necessary steps to prepare and get clearance for any research that will involve human subjects.

❑ *Certification*: Ensure all research personnel complete the free, official course offered by the National Institutes of Health.[1]

❑ *IRB approval*: Submit your application, get approved, and follow the plan you describe, including:

- Data security
- Respondent consent forms

❑ *Clear definitions for outcome measures*: Since "take-up" is a critical component in many impact evaluations, make sure it is clearly defined. For example, in studies of savings, we have seen cases where many people opened accounts but few went on to use them actively. Is take-up merely opening the account (easier to track) or account usage (harder to track)?

❑ *Piloting if necessary*: If your intervention implies any changes to "normal" operations of a partner organization, it's wise to pilot. Whenever possible, pilot with the partner, engaging their staff and systems as you would in the full study, both to help smooth implementation and to help relevant stakeholders understand the evaluation process.

WORKING WITH PARTNERS

❑ *Memorandum of Understanding (MOU)*: Create a document that codifies the agreement between the major stakeholders cooperating on an experiment. The MOU should explicitly address, at least:

- Roles and responsibilities of each party
- Definition of treatment and control
- Sample frame
- Timeline
- Rights to share findings (Though it is not the subject of this book, other researchers tend to look askance when parts of one's research are embargoed from public view. Do not cede your right to publish findings that you want to publish. It taints the rest of your portfolio.)

In our experience MOUs are not realistically legally binding documents. Their real function is to force all parties to develop and explicitly agree to a work plan. As such, an MOU should not be laden with legalese. Use plain, clear language and jump right to the important stuff.

❑ *Understanding motivations*: Take time to elicit partners' interests in doing the study. How will it benefit them? Incorporating their needs into the design of both study and surveys will deliver value and keep relationships strong, which in turn will help ensure they remain active and engaged.

  - Look for partners who genuinely want to learn *whether* and *how* their program works—and who are open to hearing that it has faults. Partners merely seeking a "seal of approval" may become hard to work with if results are discouraging.

❑ *Thorough buy-in*: Socialize and cultivate support for the project throughout the partner organization, from leadership to front-line staff in the branches, clinics, field offices, and so forth where implementation will occur. Projects that have support locally but not from headquarters rarely work; projects that have support *only* from headquarters never do.

SURVEYS

❑ *Choosing a format*: Computer-assisted interviewing (CAI) vs. paper

- CAI can significantly mitigate the risk of surveyor errors by building safeguards into the programming of the survey itself, such as logic checks and preprogrammed skip patterns.
- CAI makes it easy to prefill data (e.g., household rosters) for subsequent survey rounds.
- Data is encoded in real time with CAI, which allows for diagnostic high-frequency checks throughout the data collection phase. This enables researchers to identify troubling patterns in data while there is still time to adjust.
- Costs associated with CAI can be significant: selecting the right device and programming software, programming and debugging a survey, and training enumerators to use electronic devices.
- Reaping the full benefits of CAI requires substantial work up front to program and bench-test the instrument and develop .do files that perform the necessary checks and prepare the data for analysis. In essence, it means shifting the typical survey workflow so that the bulk of the work is done prior to data collection. If you choose CAI, you should plan around this shift in workload. (In its guidelines on choosing your data

collection method, IPA walks through all these issues in detail).

❑ *Translation*

- Any survey that will be administered in languages other than the one in which it was originally composed should be independently translated and *independently back-translated* to ensure the questions preserve their meaning.
- Creating dictionaries and identifying preferred translations for key words/terms can help improve consistency and reduce noise related to variation in translation.

❑ *Piloting your survey*

- Depending on the survey's characteristics, you may want to do up to three rounds of piloting before launch:
  - ◆ #1: Test any questions that have not been asked in this setting before;
  - ◆ #2: Pilot the entire survey post-translation (if the survey is conducted in a language other than its original writing);
  - ◆ #3: Pilot the full programmed survey (if the survey is electronic).
- Do not pilot in study areas. Find highly similar nearby places instead.

❑ *Comparisons*: Think ahead to what other results you are going to want to compare your results to. Get their survey instruments and incorporate similar language/questions where possible. But don't replicate sloppy work: think critically about each question.

❏ *Surveyor training*

- Allot at least five days for a typical household survey, including classroom and field practice (but not in study areas).
- The default should be that surveyors do not prompt respondents with answers. Be explicit about any exceptions to this rule.
- Create a surveyor manual: an annotated version of the survey instrument with all additional instructions for surveyors.

❏ *Implementing a survey*

- Practicing in the field: Before launch, build in time to observe surveyors working in the field. Two common approaches are:
  - Test run in non-study area: Administer the survey in a non-study area for several days, observing surveyors while they work and checking their outputs carefully. Communicate to all surveyors that the stakes are high—those who perform poorly should be cut (and prepare for this eventuality by training more surveyors than you will ultimately use).
  - False launch: The first day of surveying should be a mock launch, conducted in a non-study area (and the survey team should think it is a real-live launch). At the end of this day, debrief with the survey team and share lessons learned, what went well or poorly, and so forth. Note that this approach may be infeasible if you engage the same surveyors across many projects. You can only fool people once.

- Create and use survey tracking forms that record which individuals or households were surveyed, by whom, and when, who was supervising, and so forth.

❏ *Quality control*

- *Accompaniments*: Go with surveyors into the field as much as possible, especially as work begins. Spend an entire survey (or more) with each surveyor to make sure he or she understands the instrument and is administering it properly. These visits allow you to catch mistakes early on in the data collection process and use them as lessons for the entire team.
- *Random spot checks*: Throughout the data collection phase, make unannounced visits to observe surveyors while they work. Researchers' schedules often preclude having eyes in the field every day, but it is still important to monitor the whole team. It is best to randomly select whom you will visit and when so that your visits are unpredictable and surveyors cannot prepare for them in advance. This will give you a more accurate picture of how they are conducting the surveys.
- *Back checks*: Return to a randomly selected subset of respondents and re-administer specific questions to check for things like enumerator fraud and the stability of key outcome measures. IPA recommends back checking at least 10 questions from at least 10 percent of all surveys. It is important to make sure that an equal number of back-check surveys are carried out for each surveyor.
- *Ongoing scrutiny, editing the questionnaire, and high frequency checks (HFCs)*: At the end of each day (or, in some cases, each week), all newly completed surveys

should be checked for things like completion, missing fields, and inconsistencies.

- ◆ In the case of paper data collection, an editor or supervisor looks over the questionnaires for errors and missing fields.
- ◆ In the case of CAI, this process is more automated. Create .do files to run at the end of the day (or week) that check incoming data for any common errors. High frequency checks can also be used to detect patterns of behavior and performance for surveyors. For example, high frequency checks can identify if a surveyor is constantly skipping a particular section in order to reduce the amount of time spent on a survey. Information from both scrutiny and automated checks can also be tied to performance incentives for surveyors.

DAY-TO-DAY STUDY MANAGEMENT

❑ Have staff on the ground as much as you possibly can. Ongoing oversight in the form of scrutiny and data checks will catch some important errors, but there is no substitute for direct observation. Simply getting out of the office and into the field will make you aware of, and sensitive to, issues you would otherwise overlook.

❑ Keep detailed logs, including:

- How you identified your sample
- How you randomized (Keep the exact script! Do not just use Excel. It is best to be able to re-create exactly using statistical software.)

- Who did what tasks on which days
- Irregularities and issues that arose in the field

❑ Work with partner organizations to come up with a monitoring plan so they know what to expect and know what indicators will be tracked. This may include creating tools to monitor or communicate the process to partner staff.

❑ Regularly share relevant monitoring data with all partner organizations.

ACKNOWLEDGMENTS

We thank Seth Ditchik and the anonymous referees for their incredibly useful comments and guidance. Thanks also to Jenny Wolkowicki, Jenn Backer, Alexandria Leonard, Theresa Liu, Julie Shawvan and the team at Princeton University Press for helping us reach the finish line.

We thank Sana Khan for help in the early phases of this book, sifting through myriad failures and helping us categorize them and think about what we learn from each. We thank several people for reading and commenting and brainstorming with us at various stages of the book, including Laura Fellman, Rachel Glennerster, Wendy Lewis, Faith McCollister, and Megan McGuire.

For help on details of the various failure stories in the book, we thank the researchers and field staff for sharing their stories with us (and the world): this list includes Hunt Allcott, Dan Katz, Chris Blattman, Tricia Gonwa, Nathan Paluck, Rick Hornbeck, Piyush Tantia, Tomoko Harigaya, Nathanael Goldberg, Tavneet Suri, Billy Jack, Rachel Levenson, Aaron Dibner-Dunlap, Manoj Mohanan, and Rebecca Thornton. We also thank the many partnering organizations, both named and unnamed, for their engagement with researchers. Many failures for research are ultimately about tough trade-offs on operations for implementers.

Thanks to Rachel Glennerster and Kudzai Takavarasha for writing *Running Randomized Evaluations*, so that we could focus this book squarely on what not to do and guide people to theirs for what to do.

We thank David McKenzie and Berk Özler for their enthusiasm and collaboration in creating the online companion to this book (http://blogs.worldbank.org/impactevaluations /failure) to enable more researchers to share their failure stories (and for hosting the site!). Thanks also to Heidi Linz and David Batcheck at IPA for their help in putting up a website to direct people to papers cited and to further the conversation on failing in the field.

We would like to thank too-numerous-to-name friends, family members, and colleagues for generous and helpful conversations about failures—what they are, how they happen, and how to learn from them. Working on this project has confirmed for us that it is a truly universal topic; wisdom came from all quarters.

Dean thanks his family, in particular Cindy, whose love and support made the successes and failures all possible. And thanks for traveling almost nonstop every summer. Many of those trips, as this book highlights, did not lead to successful research. But some great times, that is for sure!

Jake thanks Laura Fillmore, MFA, the best person to consult about writing a book. Thanks always to Mom, Dad, Naomi, Julie, and Bear, whose love, interest, and support never fail. And to Chelsea, who—in addition to all of the above—is the one success that overcomes and outlasts all failures.

INTRODUCTION: WHY FAILURES?

1. From p. 5 of an informational booklet on the program, published by the Indonesian government (http://www.tnp2k.go.id/images /uploads/downloads/Booklet%20Penetapan%20Sasaran-Solusi%20 Kepesertaan%20dan%20Pemutakhiran-A5.pdf, accessed February 3, 2016).

2. As of the end of the 2014–15 academic year, from J-PAL's summary of the research and scale-up (https://www.povertyactionlab.org /scale-ups/teaching-right-level, accessed February 3, 2016).

3. Confirmed by IPA as of February 2016.

4. From J-PAL's summary of deworming research and scale-up efforts, (https://www.povertyactionlab.org/scale-ups/deworming -schools-improves-attendance-and-benefits-communities-over-long -term, accessed February 3, 2016).

5. Original data from Evidence Action, reported by J-PAL in its summary of the chlorine dispenser program (https://www.povertyactionlab.org /scale-ups/chlorine-dispensers-community-sources-provide-safe -water-kenya-malawi-and-uganda, accessed February 3, 2016).

6. This is classified by IPA and J-PAL as a *policy influence*: a case where research impacted policy decisions but where an exact head count requires making too many (and too uncertain) assumptions.

7. Reported in J-PAL's summary (https://www.povertyactionlab.org /scale-ups/police-skills-training, accessed February 3, 2016).

8. As of February 2016, CGAP Factsheets (available through http://www.microfinancegateway.org/library/reaching-poorest-scale, accessed February 12, 2016) detail 33 individual Graduation programs in 20+ countries totaling over 400,000 households. A large scale-up effort in Ethiopia, planned for 2016, is slated to reach as many as 3 million additional households.
9. See Olken, Onishi, and Wong 2014.
10. See Barrera-Osorio et al. 2011.
11. See Banerjee et al. 2015.
12. See Cohen and Dupas 2010.
13. See Banerjee et al. 2007.
14. See Kremer et al. 2011.
15. See Banerjee et al. 2015.
16. See Haushofer and Shapiro 2013.

CHAPTER 2: TECHNICAL DESIGN FLAWS

1. See Karlan and Wood (2016).

CHAPTER 4: SURVEY AND MEASUREMENT EXECUTION PROBLEMS

1. Consider Ghana, for instance, where it is common to have two different first names, one "Christian" and one "local." The most common local names are based on days of the week. A boy born on a Monday, for instance, would be Kojo (or Kujo, Cujo, Cudjoe, Kwodwo, etc.). A person might go by either the Christian or local name (or both), and different official documents might have different variants. Add to this a handful of regionally common surnames and it's clear that names can be a slippery identifier.
2. Two relevant summaries are Camerer et al. 1999 and Harrison and Rutström 2008.

CHAPTER 5: LOW PARTICIPATION RATES

1. See Van den Steen 2004 for a discussion and citations of canonical work.
2. See Johnson et al. 1993.

CHAPTER 6: CREDIT AND FINANCIAL LITERACY TRAINING

1. See Karlan and Valdivia 2010.
2. See Bruhn, Ibarra, and McKenzie 2014.
3. These are just two of many examples; for a more comprehensive review of financial literacy programs and their impacts on financial behavior and outcomes, see Hastings, Madrian, and Skimmyhorn 2013.
4. A discussion forum hosted by the *Boston Review* captures key perspectives on the issue: http://www.bostonreview.net/forum/can -technology-end-poverty (accessed February 3, 2016).
5. Karlan's response in the *Boston Review* forum summarizes our point of view: http://www.bostonreview.net/forum/can-technology -end-poverty/evaluate.
6. See Karlan and Valdivia 2010.

CHAPTER 7: INTEREST RATE SENSITIVITY

1. The South Africa study is Karlan and Zinman 2008, and the Mexico study is Karlan and Zinman 2013.

CHAPTER 8: YOUTH SAVINGS

1. For a review of mostly experimental savings research, see Karlan, Ratan, and Zinman 2013.
2. See a broad review of experimental work on preference- and value-elicitation approaches by Harrison and Rutström (2008).
3. This result comes from a meta-analysis by Little and Berrens (2004).

CHAPTER 11: BUNDLING CREDIT AND INSURANCE

1. In a recent review of the literature, Panda et al. (2013) find: "The penetration of health insurance in most low-income countries remains very low."
2. A World Bank article (Acharya et al. 2013) reviewed nineteen studies of insurance programs in developing countries. Though few studies

focused on take-up, the authors note some general trends, including that the quality of the underlying services offered influences consumers' choices of whether or not to enroll.

CONCLUSION

1. Quoted in Foster 2007.

APPENDIX

1. https://phrp.nihtraining.com/users/login.php (accessed April 17, 2015).

BIBLIOGRAPHY

Acharya, Arnab, Sukumar Vellakkal, Fiona Taylor, Edoardo Masset, Ambika Satija, Margaret Burke, and Shah Ebrahim. 2013. "The Impact of Health Insurance Schemes for the Informal Sector in Low- and Middle-Income Countries: A Systematic Review." Policy Research Working Papers. The World Bank. http://elibrary.worldbank.org/doi/book/10.1596/1813-9450-6324.

Allcott, Hunt. 2015. "Site Selection Bias in Program Evaluation." *Quarterly Journal of Economics* 130 (3): 1117–65. doi:10.1093/qje/qjv015.

Banerjee, A., E. Duflo, N. Goldberg, D. Karlan, R. Osei, W. Pariente, J. Shapiro, B. Thuysbaert, and C. Udry. 2015. "A Multifaceted Program Causes Lasting Progress for the Very Poor: Evidence from Six Countries." *Science* 348 (6236): 1260799. doi:10.1126/science.1260799.

Banerjee, A. V., S. Cole, E. Duflo, and L. Linden. 2007. "Remedying Education: Evidence from Two Randomized Experiments in India." *Quarterly Journal of Economics* 122 (3): 1235–64. doi:10.1162/qjec.122.3.1235.

Banerjee, Abhijit, Jordan Kyle, Benjamin A. Olken, Sudarno Sumarto, and Rema Hanna. 2015. "Tangible Information and Citizen Empowerment: Identification Cards and Food Subsidy Programs in Indonesia." National Bureau of Economic Research Working Paper #20923. https://www.povertyactionlab.org/sites/default/files/publications/553%20ID%20Cards%20in%20Subsidy%20Program%20Nov2015.pdf.

Barrera-Osorio, Felipe, Marianne Bertrand, Leigh L. Linden, and Francisco Perez-Calle. 2011. "Improving the Design of Conditional Transfer Programs: Evidence from a Randomized Education Experiment in Colombia." *American Economic Journal: Applied Economics* 3 (2): 167–95. doi:10.1257/app.3.2.167.

Bruhn, Miriam, Gabriel Lara Ibarra, and David McKenzie. 2014. "The Minimal Impact of a Large-Scale Financial Education Program in Mexico City." *Journal of Development Economics* 108 (May): 184–89. doi:10.1016/j.jdeveco.2014.02.009.

Camerer, Colin F., Robin M. Hogarth, David V. Budescu, and Catherine Eckel. 1999. "The Effects of Financial Incentives in Experiments: A Review and Capital-Labor-Production Framework." In *Elicitation of Preferences*, ed. Baruch Fischhoff and Charles F. Manski, 7–48. Dordrecht: Springer Netherlands. http://link.springer.com/10.1007/978-94-017-1406-8_2.

Cohen, Jessica, and Pascaline Dupas. 2010. "Free Distribution or Cost-Sharing? Evidence from a Randomized Malaria Prevention Experiment." *Quarterly Journal of Economics* 125 (1): 1–45. doi:10.1162/qjec.2010.125.1.1.

Duflo, Esther, Rachel Glennerster, and Michael Kremer. 2008. "Using Randomization in Development Economics Research: A Toolkit." *Handbook of Development Economics* 4 (5): 3895–3962.

Durlauf, Steven N., ed. 2008. "Value Elicitation." In *The New Palgrave Dictionary of Economics*. 2nd ed. Basingstoke: Palgrave Macmillan.

Foster, Lauren. 2007. "Coming Clean." *Financial Times*, December 11. http://www.ft.com/cms/s/0/db4dfec2-a78a-11dc-a25a-0000779fd2ac.html.

Gerber, Alan S., and Donald P. Green. 2012. *Field Experiments: Design, Analysis, and Interpretation.* 1st ed. New York: W. W. Norton.

Glennerster, Rachel, and Kudzai Takavarasha. 2013. *Running Randomized Evaluations: A Practical Guide.* Princeton: Princeton University Press.

Harrison, Glenn W., and E. Elisabet Rutström. 2008. "Experimental Evidence on the Existence of Hypothetical Bias in Value Elicitation Experiments." In *Handbook of Experimental Economics Results*, 752–67. New York: Elsevier.

Hastings, Justine S., Brigitte C. Madrian, and William L. Skimmyhorn. 2013. "Financial Literacy, Financial Education, and Economic Outcomes." *Annual Review of Economics* 5 (1): 347–73.

Haushofer, Johannes, and Jeremy Shapiro. 2013. "Household Response to Income Changes: Evidence from an Unconditional Cash Transfer Program in Kenya." Working Paper.

Johnson, Eric J., John Hershey, Jacqueline Meszaros, and Howard Kunreuther. 1993. "Framing, Probability Distortions, and Insurance Decisions." *Journal of Risk and Uncertainty* 7 (1): 35–51. doi:10.1007 /BF01065313.

Karlan, Dean, Aishwarya Ratan, and Jonathan Zinman. 2014. "Savings by and for the Poor: A Research Review and Agenda." *Review of Income and Wealth*, ser. 60, no. 1 (March): 36–78. doi: 10.1111/roiw .12101.

Karlan, Dean, and Martin Valdivia. 2010. "Teaching Entrepreneurship: Impact of Business Training on Microfinance Clients and Institutions." *Review of Economics and Statistics* 93 (2): 510–27. doi:10.1162 /REST_a_00074.

Karlan, Dean and Daniel Wood. 2016. "The effect of effectiveness: Donor response to aid effectiveness in a direct mail fundraising experiment." *Journal of Behavioral and Experimental Economics* forthcoming.

Karlan, Dean S., and Jonathan Zinman. 2008. "Credit Elasticities in Less-Developed Economies: Implications for Microfinance." *American Economic Review* 98 (3): 1040–68. doi:10.1257/aer.98.3.1040.

———. 2010. "Expanding Credit Access: Using Randomized Supply Decisions to Estimate the Impacts." *Review of Financial Studies* 23 (1): 433–64.

———. 2011. "Microcredit in Theory and Practice: Using Randomized Credit Scoring for Impact Evaluation." *Science* 332 (6035): 1278–84. doi:10.1126/science.1200138.

———. 2013. "Long-Run Price Elasticities of Demand for Credit: Evidence from a Countrywide Field Experiment in Mexico." National Bureau of Economic Research Working Paper 19106 (June). http: //www.nber.org/papers/w19106.

Kremer, Michael, Edward Miguel, Sendhil Mullainathan, Clair Null, and Alix Zwane. 2011. "Social Engineering: Evidence from a Suite of Take-up Experiments in Kenya." Working Paper.

Little, Joseph, and Robert Berrens. 2004. "Explaining Disparities between Actual and Hypothetical Stated Values: Further Investigation Using Meta-Analysis." *Economics Bulletin* 3 (6): 1–13.

Olken, Benjamin A., Junko Onishi, and Susan Wong. 2014. "Should Aid Reward Performance? Evidence from a Field Experiment on Health and Education in Indonesia." *American Economic Journal: Applied Economics* 6 (4): 1–34. doi:10.1257/app.6.4.1.

Panda, Pradeep, Iddo Dror, Tracey Perez Koehlmoos, S. A. Shahed Hossain, Denny John, Jahangir A. M. Khan, and David Dror. 2013. "What Factors Affect Take up of Voluntary and Community-Based Health Insurance Programmes in Low- and Middle-Income Countries? A Systematic Review (Protocol)." EPPI-Centre, Social Science Research Unit, Institute of Education, University of London. http://eppi.ioe.ac.uk/cms/LinkClick.aspx?fileticket=mlD5N28OmEs%3D&tabid=3174.

Thaler, Richard H., and Cass R Sunstein. 2009. *Nudge: Improving Decisions about Health, Wealth, and Happiness*. New York: Penguin.

Tversky, Amos, and Derek J. Koehler. 1994. "Support Theory: A Nonextensional Representation of Subjective Probability." *Psychological Review* 101 (4): 547–67. doi:10.1037/0033-295X.101.4.547.

Van den Steen, Eric. 2004. "Rational Overoptimism (and Other Biases)." *American Economic Review* 94 (4): 1141–51. doi:10.1257/0002828042002697.

INDEX

Page numbers in *italics* refer to figures.

157